Lost Innocents

Lost Innocents reports the authors' second major study into fatal child abuse in the United Kingdom. The book is a follow-up to their influential *Beyond Blame: Child Abuse Tragedies Revisited*, which was a comprehensive attempt to identify practice lessons from public inquiry reports into children's deaths. This second study is of a more representative group of cases which were notified to the Department of Health under a procedure known as 'Part 8' Reviews.

The authors review current knowledge about fatal child abuse and discuss an interactional framework for understanding child maltreatment and professionals' responses to it. Their findings include evidence of links with parental mental health problems, especially substance misuse, a significant under-reporting of fatal abuse, shortcomings in the way that assessments were conducted and missed warning signs.

Proposals are made for promoting the recognition and assessment of risk to children, improving liaison between agencies, enhancing preventive strategies and addressing the ethos and content of professional training.

Lost Innocents will be essential reading for all professionals concerned with the practice and teaching of child protection, as well as those responsible for policy.

Peter Reder is Consultant Child Psychiatrist in the Wolverton Gardens Child and Family Consultation Centre, part of the Ealing, Hammersmith and Fulham Mental Health Trust in west London.
Sylvia Duncan is Consultant Clinical Psychologist at Baker and Duncan Family Consultancy, Ashwood Centre, Woking, Surrey.

Lost Innocents

A follow-up study of fatal child abuse

Peter Reder and Sylvia Duncan

Brunner-Routledge
Taylor & Francis Group

HOVE AND NEW YORK

First published 1999
by Routledge
11 New Fetter Lane, London EC4P 4EE

Simultaneously published in the USA and Canada
by Routledge
29 West 35th Street, New York, NY 10001

Reprinted in 2000

Reprinted in 2003
by Brunner-Routledge
27 Church Road, Hove, East Sussex BN3 2FA
29 West 35th Street, New York NY 10001

Brunner-Routledge is an imprint of the Taylor & Francis Group

© 1999 Peter Reder and Sylvia Duncan

Typeset in Times by Routledge
Printed and bound in Great Britain by
St Edmundsbury Press Ltd, Bury St Edmunds, Suffolk

British Library Cataloguing in Publication Data
A catalogue record for this book is available from the British Library

Library of Congress Cataloging-in-Publication Data
Reder, Peter, 1946–
        Lost innocents: a follow-up study of fatal child abuse / Peter Reder
        and Sylvia Duncan.
        Includes bibliographical references and index
        1. Child abuse–Great Britain. 2. Child abuse–Great
        Britain–Prevention. 3. Abused children–Great Britain–Mortality. 4.
        Child welfare–Great Britain. 5. Family social work–Great Britain.
        I. Duncan, Sylvia, 1948–. II. Title.
        HV6626.54.G7R45   1999
        362.76'56' 0941–dc21   98–51640

ISBN 0–415–20269–8 (hbk)
ISBN 0–415–20270–1 (pbk)

Contents

Illustrations

Tables

Figures

Preface

This book reports a study into fatal child abuse which was based upon case files held in the Department of Health. The files had been submitted to the Department following local reviews into instances where a child had died or been seriously injured as the result of abuse, or abuse was suspected to have contributed to the outcome. These local reviews are known as 'Part 8' Reviews because guidance to their terms of reference and conduct are contained in Section 8 of the document *Working Together* (Home Office *et al.* 1991). Each review collects together details of the case and how members of the professional network have responded to the family's problems, followed by recommendations for improvement in procedures or practice.

Our study was intended to re-examine individual reports and then obtain an overview of a series in order to elicit additional practice lessons. It was a follow-up of a study we had conducted previously of public inquiries into fatal child abuse. We undertook this first project with a social work colleague, Moira Gray, and the results were published as a book *Beyond Blame* (Reder *et al.* 1993a). The book became a core text on social work courses, and we were also told that its practical focus enabled other trainers to use it as the basis for teaching events.

For this follow-up study, we set out to review a more representative group of cases using a similar approach. We contacted the Department of Health to ask whether we might use a series of 'Part 8' Review reports as the basis for this research and are very grateful that the Department allowed us access to their files. They also supported the project through a research grant and set up a steering committee, consisting of Kathleen Taylor, Ann Gross and Jenny Gray from the Department of Health, and two external experts, Glenda Fredman, an independent child clinical psychologist, and Jane Wonnacott, an independent social work consultant and trainer. They offered valuable advice during the study and the write-up stages. However, it is important to emphasise that the opinions expressed in this book are entirely those of the authors and should not be taken to represent or reflect the views of others. The grant enabled us to employ a research assistant and we were fortunate that a highly experienced social worker, Alison Leake, wished to be associated with the project. We are very grateful to her for the work she did in summarising the material contained in each file and presenting it to us in a readily usable form, which made our own reviewing task much easier. We also wish to thank the librarians in the NSPCC and the Imperial College School of Medicine at the Charing Cross Hospital who assisted us in obtaining the relevant literature.

The process of 'networking' at conferences and corresponding with colleagues interested in similar areas has led us into invaluable contact with a number of people who have contributed to our knowledge and thinking. These include Kevin Browne, Sue Creighton, Michael Durfee, Adrian Falkov, Chris Hobbs, David Jones, Richard White and Ania Wilczynski, to name but a few. This is also an opportunity for us to express appreciation to the many people who have welcomed us when we presented our work at conferences around the country. We have learned from their local experiences and been gratified to hear that our ideas have made a difference to their practice and approaches to training.

We are aware of the sensitive nature of our material, not only because it concerns the emotive topic of children's deaths, but because it is based on confidential information submitted in good faith to the Department of Health by local practitioners. We do not underestimate the responsibility this places on us to maintain appropriate confidentiality and to report our findings in a constructive manner. We have only included case details where this would help illustrate our discussion and have anonymised all material by using reference numbers only and have not identified the localities of any of the families. We thought that it would be useful to compare the findings from this research with other reported studies and this book includes summaries of the relevant literature.

A brief explanation is necessary about definitions, which can be particularly problematic in this field. We have used the terms 'abuse' and 'maltreatment' interchangeably but, unless specified otherwise, the focus is on physical abuse and/or neglect of children. The term 'caretakers' is often used for those adults who were looking after the children at the times of their death, since some were not the biological parents. We have been careful to use 'non-biological fathers' rather than 'stepfathers' for those male caretakers who were not the child's natural father. In order to avoid the awkwardness of writing about 'him/her', we have tried to write in the plural 'they' as much as possible. With regard to psychiatric labels, we have tried to persist with the term 'mental health problem', however cumbersome, in order to acknowledge that parameters for describing psychiatric or psychological dysfunction vary widely.

However, it is possible to be more definite about some legal terms: 'neonaticide' refers to the killing of one's child on the first day of life, 'infanticide' refers generally to child murder, while 'filicide' means murder by the child's parent.

When drawing conclusions from such a review, it is impossible to focus exclusively on issues arising from the immediate material. As practising clinicians, we inevitably call upon everyday practice experiences and discussions with colleagues. We have tried to make it evident which of our comments refer to the cases reviewed and which are more general inferences.

The write-up of this study had an organic quality, evolving over time through a number of transitional stages. Two separate interim reports were submitted to the Department of Health, one about the review process (Duncan and Reder 1997a) and the other focusing on the cases (Reder and Duncan 1997a), and our views about the review process itself were fed into the Department's consultation exercise aimed at revising the *Working Together* document. In addition, we were often invited to speak at conferences or to contribute articles to journals or chapters for other books. As a result, early versions of parts of this text have appeared elsewhere. Sections of Chapter 3, on mental health problems in the caretakers, have been published in the proceedings of the Michael Sieff Foundation conference of September 1997 (Duncan and Reder 1997b). An abbreviated version of Chapter 6, on proposed revisions to the review procedures, has appeared in the journal *Child Abuse Review* (Reder and Duncan 1998) and a modified version of Chapter 7, on whether fatal child abuse can be predicted, is published in the second edition of Browne *et al.*'s book *The Prediction and Prevention of Child Abuse* (Reder and Duncan 2000).

Finally, we wish to record our appreciation for the support we have received from working colleagues and from our families. At work, the demand that this research made on our time was accepted without reservation. Our respective families well remembered how engrossed we had been during the *Beyond Blame* project and privately shuddered at the prospect of the writing of another book that would intrude heavily into family life. Their tolerance, selflessness, interest and unreserved support have made this book possible. But we make a public promise to them that we shall not repeat such a study again!

1 Introduction

This is a report into severe child abuse, based on a study of cases in which a child had died as the result of maltreatment. The study is a follow-up of a previous review by the authors (Reder *et al.* 1993a, 1993b, 1993c) of a different series of fatal child abuse cases and the intention behind both projects was to elicit lessons that could be applied by members of child protection networks in their everyday practice.

But why study fatal child abuse? After all, the majority of child care concerns referred to social services seem not to involve significant risk (Cleaver and Freeman 1995) and, in comparison with the number of children whose names are placed on child protection registers, deaths from abuse are rare (Creighton 1992). It might be, then, that instances of fatal abuse are so unrepresentative of child maltreatment as a whole that a distorted picture could emerge from focusing on this severest end of the spectrum. Indeed, recent research studies (Department of Health 1995) have suggested that practitioners tend to overemphasise statutory investigation of referred families at the expense of more supportive interventions. Could it be that the practice of social workers and other members of child protection networks has become distorted by the occasional high profile cases of fatal abuse and that continuing preoccupation with such extreme examples is unhelpful?

We do not think so. The practice of professionals is based on knowledge about the most severe and the most unusual examples of a problem. They are trained to consider the range of possibilities that might occur in any situation and to balance the risks of a serious outcome when undertaking any assessment. Therefore, professional practice is characterised by a covert preparedness for a worst-case scenario, so that an appropriate response can be given in the rare event of a crisis, as encapsulated in the sixteenth-century proverb '*hope for the best but prepare for the worst*'.

Knowledge about fatal child abuse, then, should enable members of child protection networks to keep this rare outcome within their awareness and to be sensitive to evidence of risk. We also believe that there is probably little that distinguishes the circumstances of severe unpremeditated, but non-fatal, assaults from those in which a child dies. It seems likely that it is chance whether an outburst of violence from a parent will cause fatal injuries (Levine *et al.* 1994; Wilczynski 1997). Probably the most significant determining factor is the physical vulnerability of the child, the very young being most at risk. We would argue, therefore, that inferences drawn from cases in which a child has died can be generalised to other instances of severe physical abuse or neglect. Hence, studying fatal child abuse provides lessons that enhance professional practice in general, thereby reducing the risk of serious injuries to children.

Previous studies of fatal child abuse

There have been a number of studies of fatal abuse in this country and elsewhere. Early studies tended to be based on series of cases known to clinicians, but more recent research has been facilitated by procedures to notify child deaths to review teams or to central governments. A considerable literature has now accumulated – for bibliographies, see US Advisory Board on Child Abuse and Neglect (1995), Gough (1995) and Wilczynski (1997) – which reflects not just a professional concern to increase awareness of risk factors and to reduce its incidence, but also a social concern that such tragedies can befall young children. We shall introduce some of that literature here and refer to it repeatedly in subsequent chapters in order to set our findings in context.

Epidemiological studies

It is still only possible to estimate the number of child abuse fatalities in a population, due to problems of definition, recognition, misdiagnosis and data collection (Browne and Lynch 1995). A considerable under-reporting is acknowledged (Emery 1985, 1993; McClain *et al.* 1993; Creighton 1995; Hobbs *et al.* 1995; Hobbs and Wynne 1996). It has been suggested by Creighton and Gallagher (1988) that some 198 child deaths per annum in the United Kingdom are directly caused, or contributed to, by abuse or neglect: that is, over three a week. Wilczynski (1994, 1997) estimates an annual figure in England and Wales of 308.

Early epidemiological studies identified some associated factors, such as parents beginning to bear children early and the young age of the children killed (Jason and Andereck 1983; Oliver 1983). A literature review by Hegar *et al.* (1994) showed that the severity of children's injuries is directly related to their age, and children in the first year of life are consistently reported as being most vulnerable, with a heightened risk continuing into the second year (e.g. Schloesser *et al.* 1992; Durfee and Tilton-Durfee 1995). An increased risk has been suggested for children living with non-biological fathers (Scott 1973; Creighton 1992), although female perpetrators outnumber males in most studies (e.g. Resnick 1969; Bourget and Bradford 1990). Case studies have revealed the vulnerability of unwanted children and that behaviour such as inconsolable crying can provoke unpremeditated violence (e.g. Kaplun and Reich 1976; d'Orban 1979; Greenland 1980; Husain and Daniel 1984; Krugman 1985; Korbin 1987).

Physical abuse is the commonest cause of death, but a substantial number of fatal neglect cases also occur (e.g. Margolin 1990; Hicks and Gaughan 1995), including abandonment at birth (Bonnet 1993; Fitzpatrick 1995). High risk factors and warning signs of serious abuse have been suggested by Greenland (1987), while Schloesser *et al.* (1992) have identified an association with inadequate antenatal care and perinatal problems. Fatal abuse may be preceded by episodes of physical abuse or other physical violence in the home (Hollander 1986; Sabotta and Davis 1992), although many families in which children die are not known to statutory agencies (US Advisory Board on Child Abuse and Neglect 1995; Hicks and Gaughan 1995).

Case registers

More systematic registers of cases has furthered our knowledge. For some years, the NSPCC was responsible for maintaining approximately 10 per cent of the UK's Child Protection Registers and has published a number of epidemiological and other reports (e.g. Creighton and Noyes 1989; Creighton 1992). Confidential inquiries into all child deaths in Leeds has raised the index of suspicion about the contribution of maltreatment and demonstrated an important association with social deprivation (Hobbs *et al.* 1995). In the United States, Child Death Review Teams have similarly raised awareness about the possibility of abuse contributing to a child's death and shown links with poverty and domestic violence (Durfee *et al.* 1992; Gellert *et al.* 1995; US Advisory Board on Child Abuse and Neglect 1995).

Alfaro (1988) reviewed nine reports based on fatal child abuse case registers or panel reviews in the United States. He was only able to identify a small number of risk factors which were consistent across the cases: very young children; health problems in the children; young mothers; drug abuse by male caretakers; and criminal histories among male caretakers. Also noted were problems with risk assessments and interprofessional communication and coordination. Levine *et al.* (1994) compared data from a number of Child Death Review Teams and found that approximately 40 per cent of fatalities were the result of neglect, usually perpetrated by female caretakers, while males predominantly caused death through physical assaults. The commonest perpetrators were natural parents, followed by caretakers' partners, usually male.

Case reviews

Inquiries into specific cases have given information about the families and the professional networks involved with them. During the 1970s and 1980s, only a small number of fatal child abuse cases were reviewed in the UK using a process of public inquiry. They tended to be the ones in which professional practice had aroused public concern, such as through media attention at the time the child died or because of adverse comments by judges presiding over criminal proceedings against the parents. The Department of Health collated the principal findings from these reports (Department of Health and Social Security 1982; Department of Health 1991), yet many commentators remained concerned that the same problems, such as communication break-down, were being repeated time after time (e.g. Dingwall 1986; Hallett 1989).

We thought that a major impediment to practical lessons being learned from these inquiries was the panels' preoccupation with apportioning blame between professionals for failing to prevent the child's death. It was because of these reservations about public inquiries that we set out in 1987 to review these reports in an attempt to get beyond a blaming attitude and discover whether additional practice issues could be identified. This study has become known as the *Beyond Blame* project, after the title of the book which reported our findings (Reder *et al.* 1993a). A series of accompanying publications (Reder *et al.* 1993b, 1993c; Reder and Duncan 1995a, 1995b) has further elaborated on the project. Before summarising this study and its findings, we need first to present the theoretical framework that underpinned our approach.

Theoretical framework

We approached the project as clinicians whose practice is based on systemic and related psychologies. These frameworks and their practical applications have been well presented by Gorell Barnes (1985), Cronen and Pearce (1985), McGoldrick and Gerson (1985), Burnham (1986), Boscolo *et al.* (1987), Imber-Black (1988), Carter and McGoldrick (1989), Pearce (1989) and Stratton *et al.* (1990) and we shall only summarise the main principles here. Although the premises are derived primarily from the practice of a therapeutic modality – i.e. systemic family therapy – they have much wider application and, in our view, are invaluable for understanding everyday behaviour.

We would characterise the following principles as the cornerstones of the framework:

1 People exist in relationship to each other – i.e. 'no man is an island';
2 Context gives meaning to information about behaviour;
3 Interactions revolve around the meaning that one person has for another;
4 Communication is a function of relationship;
5 Past experiences impact on the process of current relationships.

Interaction

The model is an interactional one that proposes that a person's behaviour is best understood as a function of the social and relationship contexts of their lives. Descriptions of pieces of behaviour in themselves have relatively little meaning but can begin to be understood when the contexts in which they occurred are also known. This might include identifying where the behaviour took place, naming other people who were present at the time, mapping what they did before, during and after the episode under consideration, indicating the history of the relationships of those involved and whether there had been any significant recent changes, and so on.

As an example, attempting to make sense of why a parent has hit their child requires information about the personal history of the parent, the patterns of their interactions with significant others, events which stress those relationships and whether critical events had recently occurred. Hitting the child could then be seen as an outcome of the parent's functioning, the child's behaviour, their relationship together and interactions with others in their immediate world, such as a partner. Schmitt and Krugman (1992: 79) have described succinctly the interactional nature of child abuse:

> Over 90% of abusing parents are neither psychotic nor criminal personalities; they tend to be lonely, unhappy, angry adults under heavy stress. They injure their children after being provoked by some misbehaviour, and often themselves have experienced physical abuse as children ... The occurrence of physical abuse requires not only the particular parent but also a specific child and occasion. The child often has characteristics that make him or her provocative, such as negativism or a difficult temperament; some of the more offensive misbehaviours are intractable crying, wetting, soiling, and spilling. The occasion initiating the abuse is usually a family crisis; the most common crises include loss of a job or home, marital strife or upheavals, birth of a sibling, or physical exhaustion.

This is represented diagrammatically in Figure 1.1.

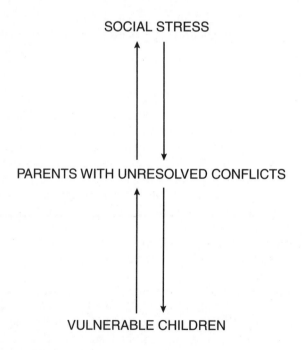

SOCIAL STRESS

PARENTS WITH UNRESOLVED CONFLICTS

VULNERABLE CHILDREN

Figure 1.1 An interactional model of child abuse

Within such an interactional model of human behaviour, individual attributes such as personality or age are only considered to be a partial description. They will have greater meaning when incorporated into a fuller account of that person's functioning in relationship with others. For instance, the proposition that young parents are more prone to abuse their children becomes more useful to risk assessments if the personal and interpersonal consequences of being a young parent are addressed. This might include whether that parent is struggling for independence from family-of-origin, or for a sense of autonomy, or whether the demands of caring for a baby are challenging their own unmet emotional needs. Again, it would be inadequate simply to regard maltreating parents as 'psychopathic' or 'disordered personalities'. We would consider such labels as convenient shorthand for a more elaborate description of the person's relationship problems and the earlier traumas on which they are based.

Personal and interpersonal conflict

Our framework recognises notions of conflict and, although it acknowledges that problems in people's psychological functioning may be multi-determined (e.g. genetic, organic or learned), personal and interpersonal conflicts are considered to have a major impact. We are not using the term conflict here to mean strife or violence between people but psychological dissonance and anxiety, based on adverse experiences from the past or tensions in significant current relationships.

The impact of past hurts, especially when experienced during childhood, makes a powerful contribution to the way people interact with others throughout their lives. A typical example might be that of an adult who experienced emotional rejection from a parent during their early years, which left them insecurely attached and anxious when close to others in later life (Bowlby 1977, 1988; Holmes 1993). Another example might be a woman who mistrusts all men as the result of sexual abuse in childhood. Hence, residues of earlier unresolved conflicts become played out in aspects of their interactions with people as they go through their lives and recurrent patterns can be noted in these relationships. Of course, individuals are not passive victims to these influences and many relationships are manifestations of attempts to resolve earlier conflicts. For instance, the insecurely attached adolescent who leaves home feeling rejected and unloved can resort to a stance of compulsive self-reliance in an attempt to overcome his or her traumatic childhood.

Psychological meaning

Individuals are perceived as having psychological 'meaning' for others in their life. Everyone grows up with hopes and expectations of those around them, whether it is a child's need for a basic sense of security from its parent(s), a teenager's desire for companionship with another or an adult's wish that someone could redress a past hurt. The psychological significance of one person for another can be influenced by different factors. These include: cultural attitudes; shared family beliefs about the world; repetitive themes in the family's history; unresolved personal conflicts; or patterns in current sets of relationships (Reder and Duncan 1995b). Hence, some meanings may be conflict-driven and unrealisable, leading to tensions in encounters with others, while others may fit with the other person's expectations and lead to a harmonious relationship.

One of the most difficult meanings for an individual to live with is an expectation that is incompatible with their own phase of development, such as a child who is expected to provide their parent with the love that they never received in their own childhood. Another is a person being attributed with characteristics that deny their own identity, such as a child perceived as 'just like his dad'.

Family life cycles

In addition to a person's functioning having crucial origins in experiences during formative years, later influences arise at points of transition in their family's life cycle. Relevant transitional phases might be the birth or death of a family member, an external trauma, such as the loss of a job or the onset of a severe illness, or phases of psychological transformation, such as adolescence and the prospect of leaving home. They are significant because they require relationship adjustments by everyone involved. Some families negotiate these transitions without much difficulty but, for others, the adjustment can be prolonged or stressful, giving rise to psychological symptoms and enduring relationship struggles. It is often when transitional change is required that problems in previous adjustments or the enduring impact of past trauma or 'stuck' meanings become apparent.

Family life cycle transitions are represented diagrammatically in Figure 1.2, which depicts a child living and developing in relationship with members of the nuclear family. The family exists in the context of the external world and interacts with social agencies, such as schools or churches, and with social structures, such as the prevailing culture

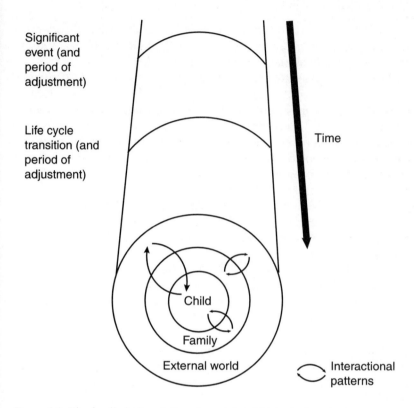

Significant event (and period of adjustment)

Life cycle transition (and period of adjustment)

Time

Child

Family

External world

Interactional patterns

Figure 1.2 The family in its relational, social and historical contexts
Source: Reder *et al.* 1993a

and the law. All elements of these systems are in continual and mutual interaction, although with different intensity at different times. These relationships evolve over time as individuals develop and negotiate new phases in their lives. Certain changes have major implications for all members of the family system, who must make significant adjustments in their view of themselves and their relationship with others. This figure also illustrates that no one element is considered as consistently exerting the most powerful influence over people's lives. Of course, certain factors may have greater importance at any one time, but an exclusive focus on, say, social pressure or cultural conflicts or intrapsychic fantasies creates a distorted explanation for people's behaviour.

Communication

Our framework interweaves tenets from communication theory with these systemic principles, because communication is both a process of exchanging information and enacting relationships.

The exchange of information between two or more people requires the use of a common language, in ways that permit those involved to relay and receive messages, to which they attribute similar meanings. Specific episodes of communication contain two components, the actual information content ('digital') and the non-verbal, emotional colourings ('analogic') that contextualise, qualify and embellish the meaning. As an example, the words 'I hate you' have very different meaning if accompanied by a playful smile instead of a threatening glare. Therefore, communications simultaneously contain messages about the information itself and about the relationship between the participants, so that, if more than two persons are involved, a group process is enacted.

At a wider level, communication is the means by which people negotiate and exchange symbolic meanings, so that it is an inextricable component of relationships. On the one hand, individuals enact their relationship through verbal and non-verbal communication and, on the other hand, the nature of their relationship gives meaning to their communications. Since relationships are not static phenomena and fluctuate over time and according to different contexts, communications, too, need to be interpreted according to time and place. The words 'I hate you' said with a playful smile can be easily understood if the two individuals have enjoyed a trusting relationship for some time, but may cause confusion if they were preceded by a series of vicious smacks or the two people were total strangers.

Episodes of communication are embedded in a number of contextual levels which qualify and give them meaning (Cronen and Pearce 1985). A specific speech act needs to be interpreted within the context of the current rapport between the participants, which in turn is a function of their ongoing relationship. This association will have evolved within the context of each person's life experiences and, beyond that, cultural parameters about how society operates.

In order that individuals can attribute appropriate meaning to the communications they receive, they must not only identify and decode the message content but also interpret the non-verbal components and relational contexts. They must take account of the tone of voice, which might reveal the level of anxiety experienced, other non-verbal cues, such as persistent eye contact, which appears to compel them to take the message seriously, evidence of preconceptions about them, knowledge about previous encounters they have had with the other person, and so on. Both participants need to monitor their conversation in order to consider whether the message contents have been interpreted as intended and whether the process of their encounter is interfering with understanding. For example, in everyday professional practice, worrying information about a family may cause anxiety in the recipient, who unwittingly withdraws and distances themselves, so that less detailed information is heard and the level of concern is diluted to more manageable proportions.

The meaning attributable to messages between two people may also be confused by distortions and contradictions that come from elsewhere. The party game in which a message is whispered from one person to another around a group demonstrates how the end result may be very different from the original content, as mishearings and misunderstandings progressively distort it. When a multi-agency network is involved with a family, the multiple episodes of communication provide numerous opportunities for messages to be distorted in this way. In addition, there are ample opportunities for communications between some members of the network to contradict messages being exchanged elsewhere, leading to confusion, partial pictures or polarised perceptions. It is evident that the more individuals who become involved, the more chances there are for dissonance between them to occur.

Further discussion about the influence of anxiety on collaboration between professionals and the coordination of the child protection system can be found in Dale *et al.* (1986), Woodhouse and Pengelly (1991) and Hallett and Birchall (1992).

Applying the framework

When applying our model to a child protection context, we have found it useful to consider cases as comprising a series of systems which have their own internal sets of relationships and interactions together. This is shown diagrammatically in Figure 1.3, which depicts the family at the centre of the professional network, with at least four significant sets of interactions operating: those within the family; within respective professional agencies; between members of the professional network; and between the family and the professionals.

Information about family relationships can begin to be organised by drawing a genogram or family tree, which diagrammatically summarises the family's structure and history (see McGoldrick and

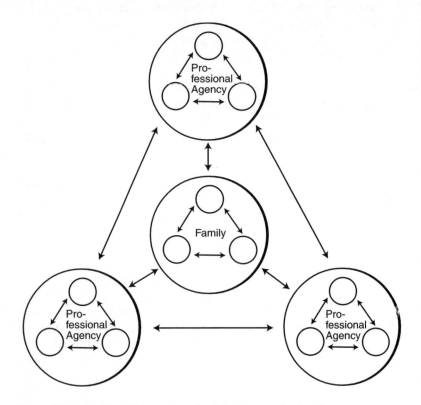

Figure 1.3 A family within a network of helping professionals
Source: Reder *et al.* 1993a

Gerson 1985; Reder *et al.* 1993a). The value of the genogram is that it also highlights important information about the family's history that is missing and needs to be sought. The evolution of the family's internal relationships, together with their interactions with professionals and the functioning of the professional network is put together through a chronology, as shown in Figure 1.4. A sequential story is elicited of the major events in the family's history, such as births, deaths, liaisons and separations, and the impact of these transitions on others. Interwoven with this history will be details of emotional or relationship difficulties manifested by family members, including problems in childcare. The unfolding story then indicates how the family problems came to the notice of helping professionals, how they responded and with what effect. If additional professional agencies became involved, the nature

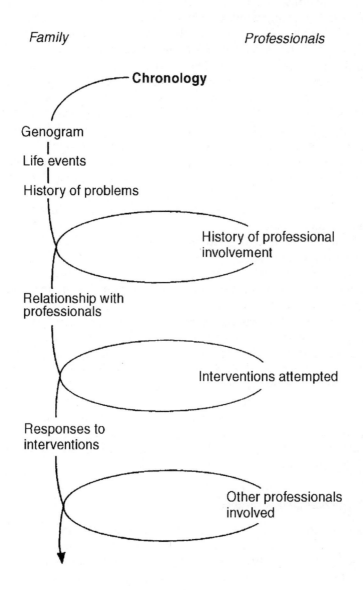

Family   Professionals

Chronology

Genogram

Life events

History of problems

History of professional involvement

Relationship with professionals

Interventions attempted

Responses to interventions

Other professionals involved

Figure 1.4 A scheme for mapping the chronology of a child protection case

of their different roles and how they communicated together needs to be known; in this way, the chronology progressively builds up a factual and interactional account of the case. Current data is able to be accorded a meaning within the context of previous information.

It is possible to identify from the chronology questions about the meaning of people's behaviour and interactions which, in turn, allows hypotheses to be developed. These hypotheses guide assessments by highlighting areas to be explored, while, in case reviews, they can be used to organise copious information into more coherent patterns. For example, if a chronology revealed that a parent had maltreated their child just after their partner had left the family, we might pose the question: 'What reason could there be for being so sensitive to losses?' One hypothesis could be that childhood experiences of rejection had led to the couple's relationship being based on strong dependency wishes which had now been thwarted. If so, it is possible that the child's demands for care were experienced as compounding the stress and resulted in abuse.

The model we have outlined does not accord with the belief systems of all professionals and it has been criticised for not paying enough attention to issues of, say, power, gender, culture, learned behaviour, 'the individual' or intrapsychic functioning. Our view is that, on the contrary, the model does respect the importance of all these dimensions but it does not promote one to a higher level of significance than any of the others. As a framework for understanding, it attempts to recognise that human behaviour is influenced by many different factors, often acting simultaneously, and an analysis of events should not be prejudiced by assumptions in any one area. Instead, a focus on the interplay of the different factors adds considerably to interpretation of events. Again, individual responsibility is fully acknowledged but, by adding an interactional dimension to it, a greater understanding is possible of what could have led individuals to exercise their responsibilities in the way that they did.

The *Beyond Blame* project

Using the theoretical framework outlined above, we reviewed reports from 35 public inquiries into fatal child abuse, published in the UK between 1973 and 1989. We recorded demographic information about each family and drew inferences about recurrent themes in the dynamics of the case. We were interested to discern patterns in the relationships within the family, in the family's interactions with professionals and in the interactions between members of the professional network, as depicted in Figure 1.3. By collating information across the 35 cases, we were able to describe a number of recurrent themes that had implications for the practice of child protection.

The families

The family genograms were usually complex, with evidence of fluctu-ating family memberships and children often conceived during temporary or unstable liaisons. Six (17 per cent) of the children who were killed were younger than one year and sixteen (46 per cent) were below the age of two years: the mean age of the children who died was 2 years 7 months. Twenty-one (60 per cent) were the youngest child, or only child, in the household. There were nineteen boys and sixteen girls in the series.

The majority of the children died as the result of a violent assault but, in addition, most also experienced significant neglect. Two chil-dren died from avoidable accidents directly related to their ongoing neglect and maltreatment, while three were shut away in their rooms for long periods and perished from malnutrition and hypothermia. A natural parent was implicated in the child's death in 71 per cent of the cases and held to be solely responsible in 54 per cent. A non-biological parent was solely responsible in 14 per cent of cases and jointly with the child's natural parent in 31 per cent.

We inferred from reviewing the pattern of their relationships that most of the children's caretakers struggled with conflicts about depen-dency or aggression that were based on adverse parenting in their own childhoods. We described these as unresolved 'care' and 'control' conflicts. Examples of 'care' conflicts included parents who developed excessive reliance on professional input, or who seemed unable to sepa-rate from their family of origin and oscillated between leaving home in a crisis and returning home again, or parents with dependency on illicit substances. Examples of 'control' conflicts included parents who resorted to violence towards partners, children or professionals as an attempt to exert power over them and fathers who showed rages of frustration when events occurred out of their control. Escalation of abuse to the children seemed to coincide with episodes of added stress in these care or control relationships, such as when a partner threat-ened to, or actually did, leave, when the mother became pregnant again or had to care for another dependent child, or when statutory profes-sionals exerted extra controlling pressure on the families.

We drew an inference from some of the cases that the child who was killed held a special psychological significance to a parent which made them more of a target for maltreatment. Sometimes this could be linked to the parent's unresolved care conflicts, such as emotionally deprived parents who demanded to have their child back from alternative care as though a piece of their property when a someone else showed an interest in 'keeping' them. Other children appeared to be associated with the emotional sequelae of traumatic family events, such as a death, because they happened to be born at the same time, while others became the conduit for their parents' marital strife. In addition, we presumed that some stepchildren challenged a non-biological father's vulnerable self-esteem because they were a continual reminder that the mother once had an intimate relationship with someone else.

Professional working contexts

It was evident that the working conditions of professionals involved in most of the cases had been extremely stressful and that this had impaired the quality of their work. A number of the tragedies had occurred around the time of a major service reorganisation or when there was a gap in service because of prolonged staff vacancies. In at least one-third of the cases, the key allocated worker was either unqualified or just recently qualified and most did not receive adequate supervision of their work. The professional agencies were frequently extremely overworked and under-resourced, with poor facilities and inadequate secretarial backup.

At a different level, the decisions of the professionals were clearly guided by social attitudes that were prevalent at the time and which were later shown to be flawed. In particular during the 1970s there was a widely held assumption that children were better off living with their natural parents because of a 'blood-tie' and this led to many being returned home from alternative care only to be reabused.

The professional networks

We confirmed the findings of many other reviewers that interprofessional communication problems recur through such cases. However, none of the inquiries had gone beyond addressing the mechanics of communication and to consider its psychology. We concluded that a number of common themes in interprofessional relationships had impacted on communication. In some networks, a 'closed professional system' seemed to have evolved, where groups of workers developed a fixed view about the case and became inaccessible to contrary information or observations. Sometimes, 'polarisation' had occurred, with a schism between two groups of workers whose points of view progressively diverged. Occasionally, certain workers were accorded excessive influence over the course of a case which was out of keeping with their knowledge about it, a process which we term 'exaggeration of hierarchy', or there was 'role confusion' when one professional adopted the roles and responsibilities appropriate to another profession. In addition, we noted that communication between agencies could be crucially impaired when the pivotal worker was absent or during a weekend or public holiday, and a number of crises occurred at such times.

We found numerous problems with the way in which professionals approached the assessment process. The outstanding theme was 'information treated discretely', by which we mean that new pieces of information about a family were considered in isolation instead of within the context of the history of the case, so that a coherent overview did not emerge. In many cases, this meant that persistent abuse to a child was not recognised or considered severe enough to warrant a protective intervention. In other cases, professionals made 'selective interpretations' of the information available to them, only registering that which confirmed a preformed view about the case and, in certain instances, these views appeared to become 'pervasive beliefs' that organised all professional responses to the family. A related concern was when practical measures or 'concrete solutions', such as rehousing, were offered as the only response to severe relationship problems that had culminated in child abuse.

An additional finding was that some parents made disguised admissions or 'covert warnings' of their abuse to the child, which professionals needed to be able to translate and assess. They included demands that the child be removed into local authority care and expressed concern for the child's health that was displaced to an innocuous problem. Occasionally these warnings came just a few days before the fatal assault.

Looking back on the study, it seems to us that the majority of our findings can be considered to be issues to do with assessment.

Family–professional interactions

We identified four main themes in the interactions between families and professionals, each of which had a significant bearing on the evolution of a case. One was 'dependency', in which parent(s) relied excessively on support from professional agencies and experienced crises when their closely involved worker was absent on leave or had left their job.

'Closure' occurred in over half of the cases, when the family shut themselves away from contact with the outside world and with members of the professional network by refusing to open their front door to them, failing appointments and keeping the child away from school or nursery. Usually, closure occurred intermittently and it was possible for us to collate together events in a case and show how episodes of closure coincided with escalating abuse to the child. In a number of instances, there was also a period of closure leading up to the fatal assault. We understood closure to be primarily an issue of control, with parents feeling that they had only precarious influence over their lives and were attempting to shut out anyone whom they perceived as likely to undermine further that sense of control.

Another way in which families closed off from the outside world was through 'flight', in which they moved home repeatedly, often at short notice and without notifying anyone. This had the effect of distancing them physically and emotionally from their family-of-origin as well as professionals and led to fragmentation of professional efforts to maintain a monitoring role.

In 'disguised compliance', parents defused professionals' attempts to take a more authoritative stance by making pre-emptive shows of cooperation, such as by presenting themselves to the social services offices unexpectedly the day before a social worker was due to make a decisive home visit. The family's compliance was only temporary, but it was sufficient to persuade workers of their apparent willingness to be more open and therefore kept them at bay.

These themes in family–professional interactions could all be understood as manifestations of the caretakers' care and/or control conflicts. For instance, it seemed to us that closure and disguised compliance were shown by adults who had a fragile sense of control over their lives and felt compelled to assert control in relation to professionals. Again, flight was characteristically shown by parents who had come from severely emotionally depriving backgrounds and we inferred that their relentless travels were both attempts at compulsive self-reliance, or self-care, and determination to keep professionals away.

'Part 8' Reviews

As we were completing the *Beyond Blame* project, the first *Working Together* document was published by the Department of Health and Social Security and Welsh Office (1988). It included guidance to local

Area Child Protection Committees (ACPCs) on how to review cases in which a child was seriously harmed or killed by its caretaker(s). This process was refined in Paragraph 8.1 of the document's updated version (Home Office *et al.* 1991), which stated that:

> Whenever a case involves an incident leading to the death of a child where child abuse is confirmed or suspected, or a child protection issue likely to be of major concern arises, there should be an individual review by each agency and a composite review by the ACPC. This includes cases where a child was accommodated by a local authority.

Local Authorities are required to notify the Department of Health immediately they become aware of such situations and then:

> Each agency should carry out an urgent management review to establish: (a) whether the agency child protection procedures have been followed; (b) whether the case suggests that there is an urgent need to review those procedures; (c) whether any other action is needed within the agency.

Each agency must designate someone to establish a factual chronology of the action which has been taken within the agency, assess the work undertaken on the case and recommend appropriate action. Individual agencies are required to complete their respective reviews within one month of the incident occurring and report to the ACPC within the next seven days.

The ACPC then has a responsibility to ensure that: 'the findings of the individual case reviews are brought together to form the overall picture of service provision in the case' and, within three weeks, to 'produce an overview report to all agencies setting out the full facts of the case, highlighting actions and issues and making any proposals for change. The ACPC should also identify any matters requiring further investigation.' The overview report, as well as the individual agency reports, are sent to the local Regional Social Service Inspectorate in the Department of Health or to the Welsh Office and must 'indicate whether there are any aspects of the case which seem to justify further inquiry, either under the auspices of the ACPC, or by an individual agency or agencies'.

The present study

We anticipated that these 'Part 8' Review files would enable us to continue the work we had started in the *Beyond Blame* project and, through studying a more representative group of cases, gain greater understanding about the nature of severe abuse and the professional response to it. In addition, we were interested in whether there were any differences between these later cases and those examined by public inquiry.

The Department of Health provided financial and general support to enable us to review their files on all child deaths or serious injuries notified under the 'Part 8' procedure over one year. The twelve-month period up to the end of March 1994 was chosen because we expected that all inquiries and criminal proceedings would have been completed and the outcome of the cases known. A summary of all submitted files was scrutinised so that we could select for closer study every case that contained evidence, or suspicion, of maltreatment to the child. Following indications by Emery (1985, 1993), Hobbs *et al.* (1995) and Hobbs and Wynne (1996) that a significant number of deaths recorded as Sudden Infant Death Syndrome (SIDS) are the result of unrecognised abuse, we were interested to include all such notifications. The selected files were then checked in order to confirm whether they contained evidence or suspicions of maltreatment and, if so, were included in our study. Examples of the cases not included were those in which a child with a chronic disabling illness died from that illness whilst in the care of the local authority.

We used the same review approach as in the *Beyond Blame* study, in which we drew a genogram of the family as it had been constituted at the time of the child's death and compiled a detailed integrated chronology of events as they had evolved. As much demographic information as possible was recorded on a research form. We then met to read together each chronology, pausing regularly to try to understand what had happened, using our interactional framework. After we had reviewed all the chronologies, we collated our principal findings across the cases.

The following chapter presents information about the types of cases we reviewed, together with demographic details about the families. More specific themes have been expanded on in Chapters 3, 4 and 5 relating to caretakers' mental health problems and unresolved conflicts and problems with assessment. In each section, we have compared our findings with other related reports in the literature. This study also allowed us to note recurrent themes in the conduct of the review process itself, which we discuss in Chapter 6. The question of whether fatal child abuse is preventable is addressed in Chapter 7. Finally, in Chapter 8, we use the findings of this study as the basis for considering training issues for professionals.

When drawing inferences from such a review of cases, it is impossible to restrict ourselves to issues arising exclusively from the immediate study. As practising clinicians, we inevitably also call upon our own everyday experiences, such as work with particular families or discussions with other practitioners. We recognise that it has not always been possible to separate inferences specific to the cases from more general observations. Nonetheless, we hope that it will be evident which of our comments refer to the study and which are wider ranging. It is also important to emphasise that any opinions expressed here are those of the authors and should not be taken to represent or reflect the views of any other person or body.

2   The cases

The information available to us in the 'Part 8' files was of variable quality and only some of them contained sufficiently comprehensive chronologies to enable us to develop detailed hypotheses about the underlying dynamics. From our perspective, an important omission from the majority of files was information about the personal and family histories of the parents, since this restricted our ability to make sense of their relationships with other adults and with their children. Furthermore, a number of reports did not include basic data, such as family structure or the ages of the caretakers. Commonly, more details were available about the mothers than the male caretakers, even when the latter had been held responsible for causing the child's death. A similar bias was commented upon by Wilczynski (1997) from her study of a series of fatal abuse cases. There was virtually no indication of the racial or cultural backgrounds of the families or professionals involved with them. Nevertheless, within these limitations, we have been able to identify a number of significant themes which have implications for practice.

Number of cases

The Department of Health received notification of 112 child deaths for the year to the end of March 1994, of which they considered that 54 were the result of non-accidental injuries or further inquiry was needed. This is similar to the numbers reported in other years, see Table 2.1.

These figures imply a much smaller number of child abuse deaths in any one year than has been estimated by Creighton and Gallagher (1988) or Wilczynski (1997). However, closer reading of the Department of Health files indicates that 'Part 8' Reviews are not an accurate indicator of the extent of the problem. First, 'child abuse' is not a precise diagnosis and parameters for concluding whether

Table 2.1 'Part 8' notifications to the Department of Health, 1990–95

Year	Non-accidental/ further inquiry needed	Natural causes	Accidental/ suicide/solvent abuse	Total
1990–91	55	35	10	122
1991–92	45	35	24	115
1992–93	59	32	14	116
1993–94	54	32	19	112
1994–95	54	29	28	120

Source: Figures provided by the Department of Health

maltreatment caused or contributed to a death are ambiguous. It is possible that pathologists and coroners are cautious about recording a death as being the result of non-accidental injuries. Second, criteria for setting up the reviews leave room for flexibility and local circumstances may lead one ACPC to review a particular case which, if it occurred elsewhere, would not be considered necessary. Third, the quality of the information available may not allow a reviewer to form an opinion as to the likely contribution of maltreatment to the child's death.

A significant under-reporting of fatal child abuse has been noted by others, including Ewigman *et al.* (1993), McClain *et al.* (1993), Wilczynski (1994) and the US Advisory Board on Child Abuse and Neglect (1995). Hence, while the 'Part 8' Review cases afford us a general picture of the problem, they cannot be taken as an accurate indication of its extent or the many different ways it can present.

Types of cases

We have already noted that there are no accurate parameters for what constitutes child abuse. While for some fatalities there will be unequivocal signs that maltreatment was the primary cause of death, there will be others in which it is only a review of the history that will prompt suspicion. Furthermore, some children may have died from a medical condition, even though neglect was a contributory factor, either hastening the death or adding significantly to the child's suffering. We have divided the cases into those in which abuse was confirmed at the time as the cause of death, those in which we had strong suspicions that the death was abuse related and those in which death was not typical of abuse, although caused by a parent. A summary of each case can be found in Table 2.2 and the reference numbers in this table are used to refer to specific cases in the text that follows.

Table 2.2 The cases reviewed

Case no.	Child		How died	Legal status	Caretaker charged		Other caretaker	
	Age	Sex			Relationship	Age	Relationship	Age

A Abuse confirmed as being the direct cause of death (N = 35)

1	1yr 5m	M	head injuries	–	m's cohab.	43 yr	mother	23yr

Child unplanned and unwanted by mother but she withdrew him from adoption in order to attempt a link with his father. Mother drifted into cohabitation with new partner.

2	1 yr	F	head injuries	(CPR after injured)	m's cohab.	27 yr	mother	20yr

Child possibly conceived through incestuous abuse and often left with maternal grandparents. Frequent incidents of neglect and bruising. Name placed on CPR between fatal injuries and death.

3	1yr 10m	F	smothered	–	mother	43 yr	father	43yr

Mother's epilepsy returned after child was born and she became increasingly resentful of her. Mother's psychotic delusions included child. Sixteen-year-old sister tried to warn professionals.

4	1 day	F	neglect at birth	–	mother	28 yr	–	

Mother concealed pregnancy. She had been ambivalent to her previous four pregnancies.

5	1yr 7m / 5 m	F } M }	smothered	–	mother	25 yr	father	31yr

Mother eventually convicted of murder. Four years previously, first child's death aged 9 months diagnosed as SIDS and most professional involvement focused on SIDS prevention programme.

6	4yr 2m	F	drowned	CPR	mother	31 yr	–	

Mother paranoid, with delusions involving the child, and repeatedly assaulted her and threatened to kill her.

7	10m	M	shaking	–	m's cohab.	20 yr	mother	19yr

Mother's cohabitee tortured child and recurrently provoked violent arguments with mother which culminated in sex.

Case no.	Child		How died	Legal status	Caretaker charged		Other caretaker	
	Age	Sex			Relationship	Age	Relationship	Age
8	1yr 9m	F	head injuries	–	m's cohab.	44 yr	mother	?

Mother's cohabitee a Schedule 1 offender who targeted prepubertal girls for sexual abuse. Child killed when her half-sister was to be interviewed by police about alleged sexual abuse by mother's previous partner.

9	4 m	F	shaking	–	m's cohab. (acquitted)	18 yr	mother	18yr

Mother recently moved from hostel to independent living, maintaining her relationship with a violent man.

10	2yr 9m	F	'massive injuries'	–	m's cohab.	?	mother	?

(File incomplete)

11	1 day	?	neglect at birth	–	mother	?	–	

Mother resisted antenatal care and child was born at home, dying immediately from neglect.

12	1yr 6m	F	ingestion of medicine	–	mother	24 yr	father	39yr

Severe neglect over a prolonged period but mother rejected social work involvement.

13	4 m	M	head injuries	–	babysitter		mother father	26yr 27yr

Siblings on CPR for neglect and children left with a number of young babysitters.

14	1 yr	F	?	–	mother	19 yr	?	

Mother charged with murdering her baby and two other children at different times while babysitting.

15	4 m	F	internal injuries	–	father	22 yr	mother	16yr

Young mother in and out of care, who looked after baby on weekdays while father looked after her at weekends.

Case no.	Child		How died	Legal status	Caretaker charged		Other caretaker	
	Age	Sex			Relationship	Age	Relationship	Age
16	1yr 11m	M	?	–	mother	?	?	

Mother suffered from mental illness for many years. Police also investigating death of mother's sister's child ten years ago whilst mother was babysitting.

| 17 | 10yr 6m
8yr 5m | F }
M } | physical assault | – | father | 34 yr | mother | 30yr |

Father history of chronic heavy drinking and psychotic symptoms, with hallucinations involving the children. Eldest and youngest child killed when sent home from school.

| 18 | 4 m | M | head injuries | – | father | 23 yr | mother | 23yr |

Professional contacts by routine health visiting. Unforeseen manslaughter.

| 19 | 2yr 11m | M | smothered | – | mother | 18 yr | m's cohab. | ? |

Mother pregnant aged 15 years. No previous social services involvement.

| 20 | 3yr 7m | F | ingested methadone | – | mother | 23 yr | – | |

Mother a heroin addict who moved frequently between refuges, squats, caravans and communes. Numerous observations of neglect and bruising to child.

| 21 | 9 wks | M | head injury | CPR | mother | 19 yr | father | 19yr |

Mother with mild learning difficulties, resented professional advice while attending special care baby unit. Plan that maternal grandmother helped mother with parenting ignored the hostile relationship between them.

| 22 | 4 m | F | head injury | – | father | 28 yr | mother | 26yr |

Father with a long history of criminal and violent behaviour related to drink and drugs. A number of observations of bruising to all children from time he joined mother.

| 23 | 1 yr | M | 'assault' | – | father | 22 yr | mother | 29yr |

(File incomplete)

| 24 | 11 wks | M | thrown out of window | – | mother | 26 yr | father | 29yr |

Mother threw baby out of window during episode of severe post-natal depression.

Case no.	Child Age	Sex	How died	Legal status	Caretaker charged Relationship	Age	Other caretaker Relationship	Age
25	2yr 2m	M	head injury	–	father	31 yr	stepmother	?

Child born abroad from an affair of father's and brought secretly to UK.

| 26 | 1 day | F | neglect at birth | – | mother | 26 yr | father | 28yr |

Pregnancy from an extra-marital affair, too far advanced for termination; mother did not attend for antenatal care and gave birth alone at home. No charges brought.

| 27 | 8 m | F | head injury | – | childminder | 41 yr | mother father | ? ? |

Parents unaware that nine years previously another child had died while in the care of the childminder.

| 28 | 1yr 8m | M | head injury | (CPR after injured) | m's cohab. | 30 yr | mother | 40yr |

Suspicion of induced illnesses by mother and a number of non-accidental injuries while in her care.

| 29 | 2 wks | F | strangled | – | mother | 24 yr | father | ? |

Mother with history of physical abuse in care and sexual abuse. Failure to thrive with first child, routine professional contacts with second child prior to murder.

| 30 | 6 wks | M | head injury | – | father | 41 yr | mother | 30yr |

Father recurrently depressed following fatal car accident. Threw child downstairs three months after physically assaulting other son.

| 31 | 2yr 3m | F | smothered | Ward of Court, Sup. Order, CPR | mother | 22 yr | – | |

Mother convicted of killing her first child five years previously, sentenced to probation with treatment. She killed second child one year after High Court ordered rehabilitation from foster care with residential assessment.

Case no.	Child Age	Sex	How died	Legal status	Caretaker charged Relationship	Age	Other caretaker Relationship	Age
32	1yr 3m	M	neglect	–	mother	24 yr	?	

Mother drug abuser and continually moving homes, refusing professional contacts. Child possibly neglected whilst mother in drug-induced psychotic state.

| 33 | 1yr 8m | F | internal injuries | – | stepfather | 21 yr | mother | 19yr |

Child's stepfather was rival for mother's attention with child's father and was known to be violent. Child admitted with scalding six months before killed.

| 34 | 11 m | F | smothered | – | mother | 30 yr | – | |

Mother unsuccessful at securing conviction against her father for sexual abuse. Probably depressed following family death and child's father leaving her.

| 35 | 1yr 10m | F | ? | – | mother | ? | father | ? |

Mother's post-natal depression included delusions which involved the child and threats to kill her.

B Abuse strongly suspicious as being the direct cause of death or a significant contributor (N = 14)

Case no.	Child Age	Sex	How died	Legal status	Caretaker/s Relationship	Age	Relationship	Age
36	1yr 4m	M	head injuries	–	father	40 yr	mother	30yr

Post-mortem findings suspicious of non-accidental injury, but open verdict returned. A previous child had died from 'respiratory failure' aged 1 yr 10 m.

| 37 | 4 m | M | pneumonia | CPR | father | 29 yr | mother | 25yr |

Possibility that mother induced illnesses in her two children, who lost weight at home and gained it in hospital. Verdict of death by natural causes.

Case no.	Child		How died	Legal status	Caretaker/s			
	Age	Sex			Relationship	Age	Relationship	Age
38	8yr 10m	M	drowning	CPR	stepfather	29 yr	mother	29 yr

Mother recurrently depressed and preoccupied with her body. Repeatedly admitted hitting child and suspicion of induced illnesses. Child wandered off and drowned; misadventure verdict.

| 39 | 4yr 6m | M | cystic fibrosis | CPR | mother | 28 yr | – | |

Child and elder brother suffered from cystic fibrosis, but child's death was clearly compounded by severe and chronic neglect of his physical needs.

| 40 | 1yr 11m | M | vomit inhalation | – | m's cohab. | 25 yr | mother | 28 yr |

Death considered 'natural causes' but there had been two previous episodes of 'breath holding attacks' and a subdural haematoma was found at post-mortem.

| 41 | 4yr 6m | F | drug induced | – | father | 25 yr | mother | 26 yr |

Verdict of 'natural causes' despite very strong indication that child was 'rented' to neighbour who drugged her for sexual abuse. Both parents dependent on drugs supplied by the neighbour.

| 42 | 4 m | M | SIDS | CPR | father | 22 yr | – | |

Parents drug abusers and repeatedly separated; child on CPR for neglect.

| 43 | 19 days | M | head injury | – | father | 21 yr | mother | 22 yr |

Post-mortem highly indicative of non-accidental injury, but not officially recorded as such and no charges brought.

| 44 | 1yr 7m | F | fell out of window | CPR | mother | 27 yr | grandmother | 49yr |

Child fell out of window following severe neglect and rejection.

| 45 | 10 wks | F | SIDS | – | father | 53 yr | mother | 31 yr |

Mother a chronic drug abuser with multiple failed treatment attempts and father a Schedule 1 offender. Child's elder sister in care and adopted.

| 46 | 5 m | M | SIDS | – | father | 25 yr | mother | 18 yr |

Unplanned pregnancy to a young mother who had miscarried and terminated two previous pregnancies. A number of previous episodes of bruising. Post-mortem showed evidence of non-accidental injuries.

Case no.	Child Age	Sex	How died	Legal status	Caretaker/s Relationship	Age	Relationship	Age
47	6 m	M	head injury	–	father	?	mother	?

Verdict of 'death by misadventure' despite strong indication of non-accidental injuries.

| 48 | 3 m | M | pneumonia | CPR | father | 20 yr | mother | 19yr |

Prebirth concerns about parenting and case conference following bruising.

| 49 | 3 m | M | SIDS | – | father | 20 yr | mother | 20yr |

Chronic failure to thrive in child and brother, who had been taken into Care two weeks before child died.

C Other abuse related deaths (N = 6)

Case no.	Child Age	Sex	How died	Legal status	Caretaker charged Relationship	Age	Other caretaker Relationship	Age
50	4yr 9m 3yr 6m 1yr 1m	F F M	fire	–	father	30 yr	mother	24yr

Mother with chronic epilepsy and dependent on father. Family preoccupied with fires and external threats. Father threatened with jail for fraud, after which series of local fires started, ending with fatal one in their own home.

| 51 | 14yr 2m | F | overdose | CPR accom- modated | – | – | foster parents | ? |

Took fatal overdose after disclosing that 17-year-old brother had sexually abused her again. Brother convicted of rape.

| 52 | 15 yr | F | gunshot | – | (stepfather then shot himself) | 44 yr | mother | 46yr |

Stepfather aggressive and suspicious man who kept guns. Professional contact concerned school non-attendance and out-of-control behaviour.

Case no.	Child		How died	Legal status	Caretaker charged		Other caretaker	
	Age	Sex			Relationship	Age	Relationship	Age
53	5 yr	F	fire	–	mother	27 yr	father	32yr

Parents deaf and dumb, with increasing marital discord accompanied by heavy drinking. Mother set fire to house after father left family again.

54	1yr 1m	F	head injuries	–	brother	9 yr	father	26yr

Brother left looking after children while father and babysitter out; brother accepted responsibility for child's death.

55	11 yr	M	carbon mon- oxide poisoning	–	father	?	mother	?

'Mercy' killing of a child dying from severe cerebral palsy.

Key

m's cohab = mother's cohabitee
CPR = Child Protection Register
SIDS = Sudden infant death syndrome
Sup. Order = Supervision Order (with care and control to mother in this case)
Schedule 1 offender = Convicted of an offence against a minor

'Confirmed' cases

In 35 of the 112 case files we examined, abuse had been confirmed at the time as the primary cause of death, either on clinical grounds or at a criminal trial. In two of these cases, two children in the family had been killed and hence the 35 cases involved the deaths of 37 children.

'Suspicious' cases

In a further fourteen cases, we believed that the available information strongly indicated that abuse had been the direct cause of death, or had made a significant contribution to it.

For example, one coroner recorded a verdict of 'natural causes', despite post-mortem findings of a subdural haematoma[40] and a similar verdict in another case contrasts with strong clinical indications that the girl's drug-dependent parents 'rented' her and her sister to their drug supplier for sex, during which he drugged them. She was said to have died from bronchitis, but the police recorded her death as a morphine overdose and her sister's urine was found to contain drug metabolites.[41]

In some cases, the child's death from a serious medical condition was hastened by parental neglect. One example is of a four-year-old boy suffering from cystic fibrosis whose parents persistently and severely neglected his dietary and medical needs.[39] We also included as 'suspicious' a one-year-old child who fell from an upstairs window following persistent neglect and rejection by her mother.[44]

We were suspicious that abuse had contributed to four deaths which had been officially recorded as SIDS. The first concerned parents who had a violent relationship and abused drugs, the mother received no antenatal care during the pregnancy and the infant's needs were repeatedly ignored.[42] The second involved a mother who used heroin throughout the pregnancy, so that the child was born with severe withdrawal symptoms, and the mother admitted having smoked 'crack' on the night the child died in her bed whilst she was unconscious.[45] The third case was of an unplanned pregnancy, followed by a number of observations of bruising to the baby and post-mortem evidence of non-accidental injuries.[46] The fourth contained a history of significant failure to thrive in both the child and his elder brother, who had been made the subject of a Care Order just two weeks before the baby died.[49]

Misdiagnosis clearly has significance for the judicial system, but also can impact on professionals' appreciation of risk to future children. In one case in which the death was eventually confirmed as being the result of abuse, the death of the mother's first child had been diagnosed as SIDS and most professional interventions and monitoring had been aimed at SIDS prevention. When her next two children were found dead, the initial concern had been that they had both died of SIDS – on the same day. The mother was later convicted of their murders.[5]

Thus, we believe it is more likely that 51 of the children (in 49 families) had died as the result of abuse.

Other cases

In another six cases, the child's death could not be classified as typically abusive. For instance, there was an apparent 'mercy killing' by a father of a child dying from a severe medical condition[55] and a man who murdered his fifteen-year-old stepdaughter and then shot himself.[52]

In our analysis below, we have separated the 'confirmed' and 'suspicious' cases if this seemed more informative.

Causes of the children's deaths

Table 2.3 shows the principal causes of death of the children, for the 'confirmed' and 'suspicious' cases. Three files did not give the relevant information. A total of thirty-one children died as the result of a physical attack and thirteen from some form of neglect. It is not surprising that the majority of neglect cases fell into the 'suspicious' category, since they included prolonged neglect of medical needs.

A number of authors have discussed how unresolved conflicts can drive mothers to deny that they are pregnant, to conceal it from others, to give birth in secret and then to abandon, neglect or actively kill the new-born baby (Brozovsky and Falit 1971; Finnegan *et al.* 1982; Bonnet 1993; Fitzpatrick 1995). We were interested to follow up these observations in this present study. Although there were three such cases,[4, 11, 26] the files contained sparse information. We did note that while the majority of cases described in the literature involve the mother's first pregnancy, this was not so for one in our series,[4] which concerned the mother's fifth pregnancy. There were indications that she had been ambivalent about all her previous pregnancies, having only presented at 26 weeks of gestation for antenatal care with the first pregnancy, considered terminating the second pregnancy, attended just

Table 2.3 Recorded causes of children's deaths

	Death confirmed as abuse	Death suspicious of abuse	
Physical assault	20	3	} 31 (61%) from a physical attack
Strangled/smothered/ drowned	8	–	
Neglect at birth	3	–	} 13 (26%) the result of neglect
Neglect	1	2	
Ingestion of drugs	2	2	
Medical illness	–	3	
'SIDS'	–	4	
Not recorded	3	–	
Totals	37	14	

one antenatal appointment with the third, had no antenatal care and then failed to attend post-natal appointments and developmental checks with the fourth. However, the file recorded nothing about this mother's early background or psychological functioning and we were left curious about the psychological meaning of children generally to her and her partner.

The children

Gender

Of the total of fifty-one children, twenty-six were boys, twenty-four were girls and the gender of one child was not recorded.

Ages

Table 2.4 and Figure 2.1 give a breakdown of the ages of the children at the time of their death. Of the fifty-one children, twenty-four (47.1 per cent) were under one year and forty (78.4 per cent) under two years. The average age of all the children was 1 year 10 months. There was virtually no difference in age between the confirmed and suspicious deaths. These findings coincide with those of all other studies, in

Table 2.4 Ages of the children at the time of their death (51 children in 49 cases)

	'Confirmed'	'Suspicious'	Combined
> 1 yr	16 (43.2 %)	8 (57.1 %)	24 (47.1 %)
1 yr	13 (35.1 %)	3 (21.4 %)	16 (31.4 %)
2 yrs	4 (10.8 %)	–	4 (7.8 %)
3 yrs	1 (2.7 %)	–	1 (2.0 %)
4 yrs	1 (2.7 %)	2 (14.3 %)	3 (5.9 %)
5 yrs	–	–	–
6 yrs	–	–	–
7 yrs	–	–	–
8 yrs	1 (2.7 %)	1 (7.1 %)	2 (3.9 %)
9 yrs	–	–	–
10 yrs	1 (2.7 %)	–	1 (2.0 %)
Totals	37	14	51

which the risk of fatal abuse is clearly far higher in the early years of life and especially within the first year.

The physical vulnerability of infants is an obvious explanation for

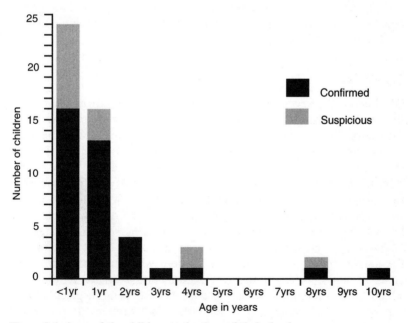

Figure 2.1 Ages of the children at the time of their death

this finding, but others may also be relevant. Babies and young infants place particular dependency demands on their caretakers because of their initial helplessness and demands for instant gratification. Persistent crying of a baby is often reported as the trigger for a parent to assault the child severely (e.g. Krugman 1985), which we discuss further in Chapter 4. Other parents find the acquisition of greater autonomy and self-assertion by toddlers the greatest stress, particularly if their own unresolved conflicts render them hypersensitive to feeling controlled by others. In addition, the birth of a (first) baby signals a transition for a mother from being the daughter of her own mother into the mother of her own child. Fathers must adjust to equivalent identity transitions. If their earlier family relationships have been traumatic, this transition can be enormously stressful to negotiate and the young child may become the recipient of displaced feelings.

The special vulnerability of babies and young infants has implications for preventive programmes. As Browne and others have argued (Browne and Saqi 1988; Browne 1995a, 1995b), preventive strategies must be carefully targeted towards the groups at highest risk to have any hope of being cost-effective. The limited resources available for prevention would appear to be best directed towards very young children, and we shall discuss later the importance of the perinatal period and the early months of life for the identification of potential significant harm to children.

Legal Status

Of the thirty-seven children whose deaths were confirmed as being the result of abuse, the names of just three were on the Child Protection Register at the time they were killed.[6, 21, 31] Two other children's names were registered between the time of their injuries and their death[2, 28] and, in a fifth case, siblings' names were on the Register for neglect.[31] One of the three registered children had been the subject of High Court hearings and was a Ward of the Court, with a Supervision Order to social services and Care and Control to his mother (who smothered him).[31] No other orders under the Children Act had been made in any of the other cases. By contrast, the names of six of the fourteen children whose deaths were suspicious of abuse were on the Child Protection Register at the time, which probably reflects the larger number of chronic neglect cases in this category. However, again, no orders had been made on any of these children.

The non-registration of so many of the children could be construed as reassuring on the basis that their deaths did not reflect the failure of a child protection plan. However, we believe that it is of concern because, in some cases, it reflected a view of professionals that the child was not at significant risk. We believe that this represents a deficiency in the assessment process, which is a theme that we shall develop in Chapter 5. In other cases, the absence of a statutory intervention was because the child's welfare had not come to the attention of relevant agencies. However, as far as it was possible to conclude from the reports, in sixteen of the 'confirmed' cases (46 per cent of the families) and eleven of the 'suspicious' cases (79 per cent of the families), the family had previously been referred to social services or the NSPCC because of concerns about parenting, a figure over the combined cases of 55 per cent. These concerns were usually directly about child protection, although some had been about a sibling and not the child who died.

Reports in the literature vary on the proportion of fatal abuse cases in which there had been previous known injuries or child protection agency involvement. Hicks and Gaughan (1995) report a figure of 14 per cent for prior injuries to the child who was killed, but this rises to 43 per cent when siblings are included. Others report 76 per cent of the families (Scott 1973), 52 per cent of the children (Greenland 1980), 'fewer than 25 per cent' of the families (Anderson *et al.* 1983), 'a quarter' of the children (Showers *et al.* 1985) and 'under half' of the children (US Advisory Board on Child Abuse and Neglect 1995). In his review of nine fatal abuse studies, Alfaro (1988) found that an average of one-third of the fatality cases involved families previously reported, a figure supported by Levine *et al.* (1994). We shall return to this literature in Chapter 7 when discussing whether fatal child abuse can be predicted.

The perpetrators

Gender

The thirty-seven 'confirmed' abuse deaths were perpetrated by twenty-one (57 per cent) female caretakers and sixteen (43 per cent) males. One father killed two of his children and one mother also killed two children.

The form of fatal abuse was different depending on the gender of the perpetrator. As shown in Table 2.5, all neglect deaths were attributed to female caretakers. By contrast, all deaths caused by men

Table 2.5 Gender of known perpetrators and causes of children's deaths (of 37 children)

Principal cause of death	Gender of perpetrator	
	Male	Female
Physical assault	16	4
Strangled		1
Smothered		6
Drowned		1
Neglect at birth		3
Neglect		1
Ingestion of drugs		2
Not recorded		3
Totals	16	21 = 37

were the result of a direct physical assault. Levine *et al.* (1994) found similar gender differences between neglect and physical assault deaths.

Ages

The age was given of only thirty of the thirty-five identified perpetrators. Their average age was 27.6 years, being 28.9 years for the men and 26.4 for the women. Four perpetrators (13 per cent) were known to have been in their teens, sixteen (53 per cent) in their twenties, five (17 per cent) in their thirties and a further five in their forties. As in other studies, this does not represent a particularly young group of caretakers, contrary to popular belief.

It has been suggested that parents who have a first child at a young age are especially prone to inflict severe abuse (e.g. Jason and Andereck 1983). We attempted to calculate this from the information available in the files but found it impossible to do so for male caretakers. For mothers, it was possible to infer from their ages and the ages of their eldest children that the average age for having a first child was nineteen years in both 'confirmed' and 'suspicious' cases, although it is quite possible that the family histories may not have been accurately reported.

Relationship to the child

Table 2.6 shows the relationship between the children killed and those charged with their deaths. A natural parent was held responsible for twenty-seven (73 per cent) of 'confirmed' abuse deaths.

These figures compare with those from our *Beyond Blame* study, where 54 per cent of the children were killed by a natural parent alone and 14 per cent by a non-biological parent alone: a natural parent was implicated in 71 per cent of those deaths and a non-biological parent in 31 per cent. In Creighton's (1992) analysis of the thirteen fatal abuse cases on NSPCC registers, seven (54 per cent) had been caused by a natural parent alone and five (38 per cent) by a stepfather or male cohabitee, while one death (8 per cent) had been perpetrated by a father and his cohabitee together. The figures are also similar to Greenland's (1987) findings in 100 consecutive abuse and neglect deaths in Ontario, in which natural parents were involved in 71 per cent of the deaths, non-biological parents in 29 per cent and substitute carers in 9 per cent. In Levine *et al.*'s (1994) comparison of Child Death Teams' reports in the United States, natural parents were the perpetrators of between 50 per cent and 85 per cent of the fatalities, the caretaker's 'paramours' for 8 per cent to 27 per cent and step/foster parents for 0–11 per cent. As in many reports, the nature of a non-biological male caretaker's relationship within the family was not always clear.

Although non-biological parents appear to be responsible for a minority of children's deaths, the picture is very different when the figures are put into the context of numbers of children living with non-biological fathers in the general population. Daley and Wilson (1993) calculated that the risk of a pre-school child's homicide from such a parent is at least sixty times higher than from a genetic father.

Having presented this overview of the cases at the centre of the

Table 2.6 Relationship between children killed and caretakers charged with their deaths (37 children in 35 cases)

Mother	19 (51.4 %)
Father	8 (21.6 %)
Non-biological father	8 (21.6 %)
Substitute caretaker	2 (5.4 %)
Total	37

Reviews, together with their demographic breakdown, we shall discuss in the next three chapters more specific themes.

Practice issues

- The contribution of maltreatment to the deaths of some children is under-recorded and practitioners, pathologists and coroners need to be alert to the possibility that abuse by caretakers could have been involved.
- The 'Part 8' procedure should be revised to enable a fuller review of all child deaths (see Chapter 6).
- Practitioners should take fuller family histories, including the background histories of the parents or other caretakers, in order to gain a more comprehensive understanding of their cases.
- Strategies to prevent fatal child abuse and neglect could be targeted at the perinatal period (see also Chapters 4 and 7).

3 Mental health problems

As part of this study, we set out to ascertain whether the children's caretakers had suffered from any mental health problems. However, we faced a number of difficulties in using the available information. Some Review reports did not accurately record individuals' psychiatric symptoms or signs, nor did they contain details of any psychiatric assessments that had been undertaken. When interpreting the clinical details 'second hand', as it were, we were left to make informed judgements about what might constitute a mental health problem. We only inferred the presence of a significant mental health problem when the available information pointed strongly to that conclusion: for example, a disturbance of thought, mood, awareness or contact with reality. However, the nature of the records does leave room for possible error. We included the category of 'substance misuse' for caretakers who had been described as showing significant and prolonged problems of excessive alcohol or drug use. We have not included 'personality disorder', since we understand that term to describe chronic relationship difficulties rather than a psychiatric disorder as such.

Within these *caveats*, the cases indicated a significant association between fatal child abuse and mental health problems in the caretakers. It is possible to present our findings in different ways and Table 3.1 first gives an overview of all relevant cases, showing whether there was evidence of current disturbance in the adults looking after the children at the time of their death, whether the current caretakers had a previous psychiatric history, or whether previous members of the household had shown evidence of significant disorder.

Table 3.2 summarises the findings for the 'confirmed' and 'suspicious' cases. In the 35 'confirmed' cases, the caretaker held responsible for the child's death was identified and fifteen (43 per cent) of these perpetrators had been suffering from an active mental health problem at the time they killed the child. Three perpetrators were clearly

Table 3.1 Mental health problems of the caretakers

Case ref.	Caretaker (*italics = perpetrator*)	Mental health problem
A Active disorder in current caretaker at time of child's death		
3	*mother*	paranoid psychosis
6	*mother*	paranoid psychosis and alcohol abuse
12	*mother*	alcohol and drug abuse (with history of overdoses and other threats to kill herself)
	father	alcohol abuse
15	*father*	alcohol abuse
	mother	alcohol abuse (with history of overdoses)
16	*mother*	undefined long-standing mental illness
17	*father*	paranoid psychosis secondary to alcohol and drug abuse
18	*father*	alcohol abuse
20	*mother*	drug abuse and depression
21	*mother*	alcohol and drug abuse
22	*father*	alcohol and drug abuse
24	*mother*	post-natal depression
30	*father*	depressive illness
32	*mother*	drug abuse
34	*mother*	recurrent depressions with psychosomatic complaints (and history of overdoses)
35	*mother*	post-natal depressive psychosis
38	mother	recurrent depressions with somatic preoccupations (and history of overdoses)
41	father	alcohol and drug abuse
	mother	drug abuse
45	mother	alcohol and drug abuse
B Previous history of caretaker in household at time of child's death		
28	mother	'mental health problems'
29	*mother*	post-natal depression
31	*mother*	psychiatric treatment after murdered first child and episodes of suicidal ideation
39	mother	episodes of depression, overdosing and suicidal ideation and possible alcohol and drug abuse
42	mother	history of overdosing
46	father	'resolved drink problem'
48	father	episodes of overdosing and psychosomatic complaints
C Previous member of the household		
1	father	alcohol abuse, claustrophobia and 'psychiatric help'
6	father	alcohol and drug abuse
8	mother's cohab.	alcohol abuse and mania
20	father	drug abuse
31	father	alcohol abuse

Table 3.2 Mental health problems of the caretakers in 'confirmed' and 'suspicious' cases

Mental health problem	'Confirmed' cases (N = 35)		'Suspicious' cases (N = 14)
	Perpetrator	Partner	Either caretaker
Paranoid psychosis	4[a]	–	–
Depressive disorder	2	–	1
Post-natal depression	2	–	–
Substance misuse	7	2	3[b]

Notes
a Presumed problem in one case where file was incomplete.
b In one case, both caretakers misused substances.

suffering from a current paranoid psychosis and this was the likely diagnosis with a fourth. Four were in the midst of a depressive disorder, of which two had a post-natal depressive psychosis, one had a severe depressive illness and the fourth recurrent episodes of depression with psychosomatic complaints. In the other seven cases, the primary problem was significant substance misuse. In addition, two of the four parents identified as manifesting a paranoid psychosis also significantly abused drugs and/or alcohol. Two other perpetrators had a previous history of psychiatric problems.

Another way to present the findings is to consider all 49 cases and include the ones where we had a strong suspicion that the death was abuse related. Since no perpetrator was identified as responsible in these 'suspicious' cases, it was necessary to look for the presence of an active mental health problem in either caretaker present in the household at the time of the child's death. As shown in Table 3.2, in the 35 'confirmed' cases, two partners of the perpetrators had also shown evidence of a current mental health problem, which was substance misuse in both instances. In the 14 'suspicious' cases, four caretakers in three families had a mental health problem, one being recurrent depression with somatic complaints and the remaining three being substance misuse. Thus, in the one 'suspicious' family where both parental figures had an active mental health problem, it was, again, substance misuse.

Overall, then, seventeen of the caretakers in 39 'confirmed' cases, and twenty-one of those in the 49 'confirmed' and 'suspicious' cases combined, were currently suffering from a mental health problem. In three cases, this applied to both of the caretakers in the household. Twenty-eight of the current caretakers in the combined 'confirmed' and 'suspicious' cases either had a previous history of significant mental health problems or a currently active disorder. In thirteen of these cases (27 per cent), the problem had been, or still was, drug and/or alcohol abuse.

Previous studies

Considerable evidence has accumulated about the effect of parental mental health problems on children in the family (e.g. Rutter and Quinton 1984; Cassell and Coleman 1995; Göpfert *et al.* 1996; Falkov 1997a, 1997b; Oates 1997; Reder *et al.* in press). The general finding is that psychiatric disorder in a parent increases the likelihood of behavioural and/or emotional problems for the child. More specific examples include links between: maternal depression and children's attachment or cognitive development; parental disorders of personality and children's conduct; and repeated parental hospitalisations and children's sense of security.

There is also a substantial literature on the relationship between adult mental health problems, especially substance misuse, and child maltreatment. However, interpretation can be difficult because of the same problems of definition that we encountered in this present study. Criteria for defining 'child abuse' vary widely and, as already indicated, many fatal cases go unrecognised. Some studies have investigated all child homicides, while others have specifically focused on fatal maltreatment by caretakers. Many research projects included all forms of child abuse, while others were confined to physical abuse. Again, a number of follow-up studies used bruising as the index of abuse, while others used whether the child was removed from the parent. Similarly, the notion of mental health problems is open to wide interpretation, with mental health professionals themselves using different parameters and categories.

Studies on substance misuse are particularly difficult to compare, since some have been concerned with drug 'use' or 'problems with' drugs generally, while others have not differentiated between dependency on alcohol or narcotic drugs. Deren (1986) has also argued that it is extremely difficult to investigate substance abuse as a factor independent of other risk factors for child abuse. Furthermore, a higher prevalence tends to be elicited from studies of maltreating parents who are known to misuse substances, as opposed to the per cent of substance misusers who maltreat their children.

Despite these problems, important and consistent trends emerge from the literature. A number of reviews are already available (e.g. Orme and Rimmer 1981; Deren 1986; Bays 1990; Cassell and Coleman 1995; Coleman and Cassell 1995; Falkov 1996, 1997a, 1997b) and we shall confine ourselves to summarising the trends and citing the more significant publications. First, we shall outline the picture for non-fatal maltreatment and then consider previous studies into fatal child abuse or neglect.

Parental psychiatric disorder and non-fatal child abuse

Many commentators are at pains to point out that formal psychiatric disorder in parents is not associated significantly with non-fatal child abuse or neglect and that psychiatric patients can and do parent well (e.g. Cassell and Coleman 1995). Nonetheless, when compared with controls, child-maltreating parents are often shown to be depressed (see Falkov 1997b) or to have a history of attempted suicide (Roberts and Hawton 1980; Hawton *et al.* 1985). Taylor *et al.* (1991) and Murphy *et al.* (1991) examined the records of 206 serious physical abuse and neglect cases brought before the Boston Juvenile Court. They found clear evidence of a severe affective disorder in one or both of the parents in 14 per cent of cases, a psychotic disorder in 13 per cent and firm evidence of substance misuse in 43 per cent (this figure rose to 50 per cent if suspicions of substance misuse were included). Glaser and Prior (1997) reviewed the cases of all children whose names were on Child Protection Registers for emotional abuse in four English local authorities. Parental mental illness, including depressive psychosis, schizophrenia, anorexia nervosa and suicidal attempts, was present in 31 per cent of cases and substance misuse in 26 per cent.

Parental mental health problems figure as a factor on a number of research-based risk checklists. Browne has undertaken prospective evaluation of a twelve-item checklist for child abuse and neglect potential and determined by discriminant function analysis the order of relative importance of risk characteristics. A 'history of mental illness, drug or alcohol addiction' was fifth in importance behind such factors as 'history of family violence' and 'single or separated parent' (Browne and Herbert 1997). In an equivalent study in Greece, Agathonos-Georgopoulou and Browne (1997) found 'parents with mental health problems' to be one of five high predictors of future child maltreatment. Egan *et al.* (1990) also found that 'past or present psychiatric treatment' predicted future major parenting problems by mothers.

The parental 'stress' that is repeatedly identified as a risk factor for child abuse is substance abuse (e.g. Whipple and Webster-Stratton 1991) and it is included as a factor on many high-risk checklists (e.g. Greenland 1987; Armstrong and Wood 1991). We shall therefore examine this problem in greater detail.

Parental substance misuse and non-fatal child abuse

Even though early studies began to demonstrate some association between drug and alcohol misuse and child maltreatment, commentators were cautious about drawing firm inferences. For example, Young (1964) reported that severe and chronic drinking was a primary family problem in 60 per cent of child and abuse and neglect cases. In their review of reports up to the end of the 1970s, Orme and Rimmer (1981) found that between 12 per cent and 65 per cent of those identified as child abusers were alcoholics, but the methodological problems in the studies were considered to be so serious and the definitions of alcoholism so varied that little confidence could be placed in their conclusions. However, based on these data, 'one cannot eliminate the possibility of a correlation between child abuse and alcoholism (or problem drinking)' (Orme and Rimmer 1981: 275).

Many more studies have been reported since then, with consistent patterns arising from follow-up research of children born to drug-dependent mothers and exposed to drugs *in utero*. Olofsson *et al.* (1983) followed up children born to opiate- and methadone-addicted mothers for up to ten years and found that 43 per cent had been removed from their mother's care by the courts, at a mean age of 15 months. Kelley (1992) found a very significant association between maternal substance abuse and subsequent child maltreatment of sufficient seriousness to necessitate removal of the children from their parents by child protection services. Jaudes *et al.* (1995) concluded that their results were 'highly suggestive that children born to women abusing illicit substances during pregnancy are at a very high risk for abuse or neglect in the future'.

By examining cases of serious child abuse or neglect brought before the courts, Famularo *et al.* (1986) report that 52 per cent of such families had at least one parent with a history of alcoholism. Murphy *et al.* (1991) found that a documented problem with either alcohol or drugs by at least one parent was present in 43 per cent of cases and the children of such parents were significantly more likely to be permanently removed into alternative care. In the investigation by Famularo *et al.* (1992), 70 per cent of the physically abusing parents whose children were removed from their care by courts abused alcohol and 51 per cent abused cocaine.

Most investigations of substance abusers who remain in treatment programmes have suggested a better outlook, although Black and Mayer (1980) found that physical or sexual child abuse, or child neglect, occurred in 41 per cent of the families with an alcohol- or opiate-addicted parent, even though the parent was still in treatment. However, Lawson and Wilson (1980) concluded that 36 per cent of children born to mothers addicted to narcotics were no longer in their mother's care by the end of their first year but those mothers who relinquished care were less likely to be using drug treatment facilities. Wilson (1989) also found that the infants of untreated heroin-addicted mothers were significantly less likely to remain in their mother's care than those of methadone-maintained mothers. Burns *et al.* (1996) found no difference when compared with controls in the health and development of 23 children born to mothers who abused opiates during pregnancy and who remained on methadone maintenance: however, four of the subject children were living in substitute care. Despite substance abuse being 'rampant' in Murphy *et al.*'s sample of parents brought before the juvenile court for serious child abuse (1991: 209), the authors offer their clinical experience that 'parents who do stop abusing substances are likely to go on to other success in caring for their children'.

Previous studies of fatal abuse

Our own findings of an association between fatal abuse and parental mental health problems, especially substance misuse, is consistent with other reports in the literature. Resnick (1969) reviewed the world literature for cases of child murder by parents and made his own re-evaluation of the parents' psychiatric diagnoses, based on the reported material: 67 per cent of the murdering mothers were classified as psychotic and 44 per cent of the fathers, while depression was evident in 71 per cent of the mothers and 33 per cent of the fathers.

In the United Kingdom, d'Orban (1979) reported on 89 women imprisoned for actual or attempted murder of their children: 24 (27 per cent) were diagnosed as mentally ill, including 14 (16 per cent) with psychosis. Overall, 13 (54 per cent of the mentally ill) had attempted suicide immediately after the offence and 10 (42 per cent of the mentally ill) were in treatment or aftercare at the time. McGrath (1992) collated details about 280 maternal filicide patients admitted to Broadmoor Special Hospital over a fifty-year period. The diagnosis was affective psychosis in 46 per cent of cases and schizophrenia in 37 per cent. Among a sub-group of 115 offenders, only four had a history of drink or drug abuse and only two appeared to be under the influence of substances at the time of the offence. The only discrepant report is from Scott (1973), who studied 29 fathers, or father substitutes, who had killed a child. None was considered mentally ill at the time of the offence and none was significantly intoxicated with alcohol or drugs.

There have been two important recent studies of fatal child abuse in the UK which have addressed mental health problems of the caretakers, one by Falkov (1996) and the other by Wilczynski (1995, 1997). Falkov, a child psychiatrist, was invited by the Department of Health to review 100 'Part 8' cases specifically to investigate whether there was an association with adult psychiatric problems. There was only minimal overlap between his cohort of cases and the series we studied. Falkov had to overcome the same problems of definition and quality of available information as we did. Although he presented his findings using somewhat different diagnostic categories, the overall pattern is very similar to ours. He concluded that there was clear evidence of psychiatric morbidity in one or both of the child's caretakers in at least 32 per cent of cases, while there was insufficient information to form a judgement in a further 23 per cent. The primary diagnoses are shown in Table 3.3. Falkov found that twenty-five of the perpetrators currently suffered from a psychiatric disorder, as did ten of their partners.

Table 3.3 Parental psychiatric disorders in 100 'Part 8' Review cases studied by Falkov (1996)

Psychiatric disorder	In perpetrator	In partner
Psychosis (other than puerperal)	9	–
Puerperal psychosis	1	–
Depression (other than post-natal)	5	3
Post-natal depression	–	3
Personality disorder	5	1
Drug dependency	2	2
Munchausen syndrome-by-proxy	2	–
Anorexia nervosa	–	1
Unknown	1	–
Totals	25	10

Although substance misuse does not figure so prominently in Falkov's findings of primary diagnoses, alcohol dependency was a secondary problem for four of the perpetrators and drug dependency for one perpetrator. One partner also suffered from alcohol dependency as a secondary problem.

Wilczynski's (1995, 1997) 'English' study investigated records of all cases of homicide of a child under the age of 18 years by a parent or parent substitute in England and Wales which had been referred by police to the Director of Public Prosecutions during 1984. As a criminologist, Wilczynski had a particular interest in the legal and social aspects of the cases but she also included information on the families, including evidence of mental health problems of the accused. A particular concern of Wilczynski has been that mothers who kill their children have traditionally been regarded as 'mad', while male killers are considered to be 'bad' (1991). In the 48 cases she studied, 48 per cent of the suspects had received psychiatric treatment prior to the offence, only a slightly greater proportion of them being females. Previous suicidal attempts were recorded in 31 per cent of cases, with a higher proportion being women. Not all of the accused parents had been medically or psychiatrically assessed but, extrapolating from Wilczynski's figures, a current psychiatric disorder was present in 50 per cent of cases and there was a significantly higher proportion of women than men thus diagnosed. The most common disorders were psychosis (in 24 per cent of the parents) and depression (also 24 per cent). Puerperal psychosis was diagnosed in only two of the six female cases of psychosis. Although definitions of substance abuse were not given, a history of substance 'use' was recorded in 60 per cent of cases, while 33 per cent of accused parents had used alcohol or illegal or prescription drugs at the time of the crime. Interestingly, concern about parental mental health had been the commonest reason for any prior contact between the families and professional agencies.

A similar picture is apparent in other countries. A study of fatal child abuse and neglect in New York City by Fontana (quoted by Deren 1986) found that in eleven of 45 cases the mother had been a drug addict and, although six of them had been enrolled in methadone treatment, most had been non-compliant. A subsequent similar review in New York by Besharov and others (quoted by Bays 1990) revealed that, in over a quarter of cases, drug involvement by the caretakers had contributed directly to the cause of the child's death. Alfaro (1988) synthesised nine state studies from the 1980s. The rate of parental mental illness identified varied between 8 per cent and 36 per cent and that for substance abuse in at least one caretaker varied widely, being

14 per cent in one study and 43 per cent in another. When fatal and non-fatal abuse were compared in the New York analysis, drug addiction among fathers or father substitutes was statistically significantly higher in the fatal cases.

In Iowa, Margolin (1990) compared 48 child fatalities from physical abuse with 34 from neglect. A caretaker's psychosis or clinical depression did not appear to play a conspicuous role in fatalities from neglect but four deaths from abuse were associated with extreme mental illness. One mother killed her child in response to command hallucinations, another mother drowned her infant because she believed God ordered her to do so and a father believed his child was possessed by demons. Four other physical abuse deaths were associated with the parent's own suicide.

Out of 35 cases of maternal filicide in Hong Kong, 14 per cent of the mothers were diagnosed as suffering from schizophrenia at the time of the offence, 23 per cent from a psychotic depression and 26 per cent from neurotic depression (Cheung 1986). Overall, 34 per cent of the mothers had previously received psychiatric treatment. Wilczynski (1997) also reported on a study in New South Wales of child homicides, where 36 per cent of the perpetrators had a diagnosis of some psychiatric disorder, 27 per cent had previously received psychiatric treatment and 14 per cent had used substances immediately before the crime. By contrast, Greenland (1987) concluded that only 10 per cent of fatal abusers in Ontario were suffering from a mental illness, which was severe psychosis in all instances.

Neonaticide is consistently shown to be a different phenomenon from other forms of infanticide, with very few of the mothers showing evidence of formal psychiatric disorder. The world literature reviewed by Resnick (1970) revealed only 17 per cent of such mothers had been psychotic and only 9 per cent were considered to have been depressed. Eleven of the 89 incarcerated mothers studied by d'Orban (1979) had killed their newborn child and the only disorders discovered were personality disorder in two of them and subnormality in one. In Cheung's study in Hong Kong (1986), there had been six cases of neonaticide by mothers, four of whom had not shown evidence of a psychiatric illness, one had a psychotic depression and one a neurotic depression. Wilczynski's English study (1997) went on to find 18 neonaticides among a total of 65 child deaths, in none of which did the mother appear to show evidence of a significant psychiatric disturbance. These findings are supported by case studies of young mothers who had denied their pregnancy and abandoned or killed their newborn infant (e.g. Brozovsky and Falit 1971; Finnegan *et al.* 1982; Bonnet 1993; Fitzpatrick 1995).

Children's vulnerability

In our study of the 'Part 8' cases, we were interested whether the nature of the children's vulnerability to their parents with mental health problems could be discerned. Although the information available in the files was limited, we are able to draw tentative inferences and suggest possible common threads to them.

Table 3.4 shows the ways that parents with mental health problems killed their children and one feature is that the offending caretaker was always one of the child's natural parents.

In addition, it seems that parents with a paranoid or depressive disorder often had made previous threats to kill their child and ultimately did so in a premeditated fashion, albeit while their thought processes were disturbed. We formed the impression that the children had episodically become central to the parents' preoccupations, including being incorporated into their delusional thinking. The final assaults appeared to be attempts by the parents to rid themselves of the perceived threat from the children.

One mother began talking to her infant as though the child had become her own mother – in other words, as though she had turned into the grandmother, who was already dead. The mother went on to make overt threats to kill her child and she eventually strangled her when she was 20 months old.[3]

The father in another family was diagnosed as suffering from an alcohol-induced paranoid illness four years before he killed two of his children. During this time, he experienced auditory hallucinations telling him to sexually molest his children. However, he aggressively shunned all attempts at treatment.[17]

Another mother, with a prolonged post-natal depressive psychosis, eventually killed her child when 20 months old. Her delusions included a belief that the daughter was a reincarnation of her own mother and she repeatedly threatened to kill the child.[35]

Table 3.4 Caretakers' mental health problems in relation to cause of children's deaths

Case ref	Caretaker's mental health problem	Cause of death	Previous recorded maltreatment
3	paranoid mother	smothered	previous threats to kill her children
6	paranoid mother	drowned	repeated episodes of bruising and threats to kill her child
16	? paranoid mother	?	possible killing of another child while babysitting ten years previously
17	paranoid father (secondary to alcohol misuse)	violent assault	previous episodes of bruising to children
24	post-natally depressed mother	threw child out of window	–
30	depressed father	threw child downstairs	previous assault on child's elder brother
34	depressed mother	smothered	–
35	post-natally depressed mother	?	previous threats to kill her child
12	substance abusing mother	ingestion of drugs	severe neglect
15	substance abusing father	violent assault	–
18	substance abusing father	violent assault	–
20	substance abusing mother	ingestion of drugs	repeated neglect and bruising to child
21	substance abusing mother	violent assault	–
22	substance abusing father	violent assault	previous bruising to child
32	substance abusing mother	neglect	neglect of child's health needs

Other children appeared to intrude more actively into their parents' thoughts and preoccupations, as illustrated by a depressed father who threw his youngest child down the stairs.[30] This case will be summarised through an abbreviated chronology, starting in the father's adulthood since, unfortunately, no details were given in the report about his upbringing and earlier relationships.

Father aged 27	He leaves work to care for his disabled parents.
Summer of that year	
	Father involved in fatal road traffic accident while driving his parents in his car.
Father aged 32	He is admitted to hospital with depression.
Father aged 33	He is readmitted with depression.
Father aged 37	He is readmitted with depression.
Father aged 41	Father's mother dies.
Father aged 43	Father's father dies.
Father aged 44	Father and mother (aged 23) cohabit. Mother notices that the father becomes depressed every subsequent summer, saying that he caused the road traffic accident deliberately.
Father aged 45	First son born.
Father aged 46	Second son born.
Father aged 51, July	Mother seven months pregnant. Father depressed again, treated at home. Three days later, mother finds him spinning and shaking one of the children. Psychiatric and social work mental health assessments performed and father admitted informally for four weeks. Social Services Children and Families Department informed but decide to take no further action.
8 September	Third son born. Midwife and health visitor unaware of earlier incident with other child.
13 September	Father writes to his psychiatrist apologising for missing a drop-in club meeting and informing him of son's birth.
10 October	Father writes to psychiatrist apologising for missing a drop-in club meeting and saying his wife had been involved in a road traffic accident.
19 October	Father seen in psychiatric out-patients, depressed, but declines visit by community psychiatric nurse. Parents register son's birth.
20 October	Father throws 6-week-old baby down stairs after shouting at another of the children for crying. He tells police he had an uncontrollable urge to get the children out of his way.

The father was convicted of manslaughter and detained at a special hospital.

We inferred a different pattern in families where the parents were substance misusers. Here, the parents were absorbed with their own preoccupations and personal needs to the exclusion of the children's. Their lifestyles were very self-centred, so that the children's safety and welfare were not prioritised. They often showed 'flight' from contact with helping agencies, placed the children with numerous unsuitable caretakers and demonstrated other neglectful behaviour. The children ultimately died from either an avoidable accident as the result of persistent neglect or were assaulted when they asserted their own needs.

In one case, the child's father regularly abused drugs and the mother was a chronic heroin addict. The couple's relationship was unstable and characterised by violence and repeated separations. There were at least two referrals expressing concern about the parents' drug taking and its effect on the child, one to the health visitor and the other to the NSPCC. However, this second referral was passed on to the health visitor and no statutory assessment was made. A few days later, the 2½-year-old girl was taken to hospital, having ingested methadone. Although the hospital social worker commented to the mother about her life-style affecting her capacity to meet the child's needs, the principal assessment was of the child's physical state and she was discharged from hospital the next day. Over the next sixteen months, the mother repeatedly moved with her daughter to a refuge, temporary homes and squats and then to a caravan. During that time, there was evidence that the mother spent most of her money on drugs and her life was chaotic. The child may have been sexually abused by a stranger in a toilet and was noted to be bruised, while her mother increasingly left her with different people. The child died aged 3 years 7 months after ingesting her mother's methadone.[20]

Making sense of the findings

How can we integrate the findings from our study and those previously reported in the literature? We suggest that debates about whether abusing parents are psychopathic or have personality disorders add little to our understanding of the problem and, indeed, it could be argued that all abusers must suffer from some form of psychological dysfunction. For us, it is more useful to try to make sense of the nature and origins of those psychological problems and this we have attempted in the following chapter. In addition, as Falkov (1997a) emphasises, parental psychopathology should be seen as one component in an interlocking web of influences associated with child maltreatment. However, it is significant whether severe psychiatric disorders such as depression or psychosis are associated with child maltreatment in general or fatal abuse in particular.

Based on extensive clinical experience, Steele (1980) considered that formal psychiatric disorder was no higher among child abusing parents than in the general population. Oates (1997: 24) concluded that 'there is little evidence that patients suffering from severe mental illness (schizophrenia and bipolar disorder) are more at risk than the general population of physically abusing their children ... In contrast, a significant minority of adults who murder their children are seriously mentally ill, particularly mothers.' McGrath (1992: 295) has warned that, though maternal filicide is uncommon, practitioners 'should bear in mind the risks to the child of a mother with a family and personal history of mental illness, who is herself showing signs of illness, and who is preoccupied with the physical or spiritual well-being of the child'.

Our own reading of the evidence is more guarded. Parental mental health problems do seem to be associated with increased risk of child maltreatment in general and clinicians need to be sensitive to the welfare of children of psychiatric patients. This is well illustrated by the three patients discussed by Mogielnicki *et al.* (1977) who had presented to casualty departments with psychosomatic complaints such as chest pain, limb weakness, headaches and visual blurring. Psychiatric interviews revealed that they feared being violent to their children or actually were inflicting harm on them. Falkov (1977c) also noted the significance of psychosomatic symptoms, even if they do not reach the criteria for a formal diagnosis of somatising disorder. Falkov further considered that the triad of depression, substance abuse and personality disorder carried a particularly poor prognosis with regard to severe child abuse.

Substance misuse is even more strongly associated with child maltreatment generally, and with fatal abuse in particular, than the other mental health problems. It appears to be the lifestyle that often accompanies relentless illicit drug use that impacts so adversely on child care (e.g. Swadi 1994). However, successful treatment can be a significant protective factor.

The literature suggests that cases in which a parent with a severe psychiatric disorder, such as a depressive illness or psychosis, kills their child are somewhat different from other instances of fatal child abuse. The parent concerned is more likely to be the mother, although mentally disordered father figures also kill. Such parents have less obvious histories of being maltreated in their own childhood, the child victims are usually older and there tend to be fewer prior documented instances of abuse leading up to the child's death. The means of killing tends to be smothering, strangling or attacking with a blunt instrument rather than punching or hitting, suggesting that there is more intention to kill by such parents. Our own figures are possibly too small to draw clear comparisons between the two types of cases, but they seem to be consistent with these inferences.

We would endorse Husain and Daniel's (1984) and Cassell and Coleman's (1995) emphasis on how often the victimised child of a psychotic parent becomes part of their delusional thinking. Furthermore, sometimes substance-induced disinhibition further impairs impulse control in parents whose judgement is already disturbed by psychiatric illness (Campion *et al.* 1988).

Neonaticide stands out as a phenomenon distinct from other forms of filicide. It involves young mothers who, although suffering from considerable emotional turmoil which leads to denial of the pregnancy, do not show evidence of a formal psychiatric disorder.

Assessment paralysis

Another process issue arose from our study. The presence of parental mental health problems appeared to have a major impact on the functioning of members of the child protection networks involved with the families, which we have termed 'assessment paralysis'. We mean by assessment paralysis an apparent impasse in the professional network which interfered with thinking about the needs of the child alongside those of the parent. This usually occurred when the parent showed delusional thinking with irrational behaviour, or evidence of a depressive illness. Professional concern became focused on whether the parent did, or did not, have a diagnosable psychiatric disorder. While this concern was clearly relevant, because it determined whether that parent needed admission to a psychiatric hospital, under a Section of the Mental Health Act if necessary, it became the factor which decided whether *any* intervention was possible. Once the general practitioner or psychiatrist considered that the parent was not showing evidence of a psychiatric disorder, members of the child protection network seemed unable to assert that the parent's behaviour was so bizarre or so dangerous that, no matter what label was put to it, the child needed protection from it.

One mother, who eventually smothered her 20-month-old child, developed delusions that her husband was trying to kill her and that dogs were a reincarnation of her dead mother. She began talking to the child as though she were the dead (grand-) mother and first threatened to kill her when she was just 4 weeks old. Her older child recurrently presented to the general practitioner with psychosomatic complaints, informed a GP trainee of her mother's delusions and visited social services to say how concerned she was about her mother's mental health. Assessments that were undertaken were of the mother's mental state. However, she always appeared calm when the GP visited. A social work assessment also focused on the mother's mental state and whether she would allow contact with professionals and did not include an appraisal of the risk of harm to the child.[3]

Knowledge that the mother was threatening to kill the 4-week-old infant was an opportunity to prioritise child protection issues rather than the mother's psychiatric state. Instead, the risk to the child was not given the appropriate priority and thereafter always came second in significance.

There had been long-standing concerns about the mental state of another mother, who eventually drowned her daughter when she was 4 years old. This mother had a history of school non-attendance, anorexia nervosa and stealing during childhood, was physically abused by her own mother and had been taken into care as a 15-year-old after setting fire to her parents' home. She became pregnant the following year and went on to have four children but the three eldest were placed with other caretakers. Her adult psychiatric history began when she was aged 23 with deliberate self-harm, attempting to set fire to her flat and admitting that she wanted to smother her child. Over the next eight years, the mother presented repeatedly with depression, paranoid ideas and threats to kill her children, herself, her parents or professionals. She was observed breaking down her front door, throwing household items and rubbish over the balcony, shouting and screaming incoherently and claiming that people were following her and coming to cut her head off. She twice locked herself and her daughter in the flat and on one of these occasions was seen at a window brandishing a knife. During this time, there were five referrals for domiciliary psychiatric assessments but each one concluded that she was not showing evidence at the time of a formal psychiatric disorder and there were no grounds for invoking the Mental Health Act. This conclusion was accompanied by a decision that no further action could be taken.[6]

Clearly, two parallel assessments are necessary in such cases, one of the parent's psychiatric state and one of the safety of the child. While they usually bear some relation to each other, they are also distinct issues in their own right. The essential point is that an adult's capacity to parent is not determined by whatever diagnosis is, or is not, used to explain their behaviour. Risk of harm to a child comes from the parent's *behaviour* itself, not from their psychiatric *diagnosis* as such. The diagnosis may guide the choice of treatment offered to the adult and may indicate their long-term prognosis and liability to behave in a similar way in the future. It does not determine the immediate risk of harm to the child. A child's safety should be determined by the nature of the parent's *behaviour* and this in itself may be sufficient to guide whether protective action is necessary. Assessments need to consider issues from the perspectives of the adult and the child and the differing needs of each may require different decisions and interventions.

The case of the father with a severe depressive illness, who threw one of his children down the stairs and killed him, also highlights the need for children's welfare to be considered alongside that of their parent.

Even though the father had physically assaulted the child's elder brother three months earlier, all professional concerns remained focused on the father's welfare and the risk to the children was never directly assessed.[30]

Post-natal depression is generally well recognised as posing risk to the baby, which may account for only one such case appearing in our group of cases. Significantly, it was one in which priority was given to monitoring the risk of the mother to herself, rather than to the baby.

> The 11-week-old baby was thrown from a window and killed by his mother during a period of severe post-natal depression. Two weeks after his birth, the mother had tried to jump from the top of a building but her family declined hospital admission, saying that they could keep a watch on the mother. Nothing is recorded in the file about considerations for the safety of the child.[24]

We have already discussed that the risk of harm to children is severe if they are incorporated in the parent's delusional thinking. If a formal psychiatric diagnosis cannot be made at the time, the risk to the child still needs to be based upon the nature of the parent's behaviour, thoughts and feelings over time. As we shall illustrate further in Chapter 5, statements like 'I want to kill my child' indicate major risk, whether or not that statement arises in the context of a psychotic state.

'Think family'

Our findings, together with others reported in the literature, reinforce the need for greater liaison between adult and child services, both within and between health and social services. As a result of the early specialisation which now occurs in professional careers, practitioners tend to be relatively uninformed about the other age group and unable to consider problems from the perspectives of children *and* adults. Each specialist service tends to remain focused on their specific client group and concerned to do the best to meet their needs. However, this often means that adult mental health service workers focus on their patients as individuals and may not even be aware of the number and ages of children in the family. Adult Psychiatry Care Programme Approach forms, intended to facilitate follow-up of patients in the community, sometimes do not contain space for data about children (Reder and Duncan 1997b). Professionals who work with children, on the other hand, have a tendency to criticise parents for failing to prioritise their children's needs and can be insensitive to the concerns of their adult service colleagues when confronted with dilemmas about confidentiality.

There is a need for much greater sharing of knowledge between adult and child mental health services (Reder *et al.*, in press). This should start during undergraduate training and continue in later professional practice, through regular teaching events which address issues across the age barrier. In addition, training in, and experience of, conjoint family therapy approaches could help widen the thinking of all practitioners so that it becomes automatic to take account of the experiences of other family members and to consider their interrelationships. For example, the impact on children of one parent's psychological disturbance can be ameliorated by the presence of another supportive adult, whether within the family or as the result of referral to an appropriate professional.

The organisation of specialist services could also facilitate closer liaison between child and adult resources. Falkov and Davies (1997) have reported a successful collaboration between child and adult psychiatrists, which includes joint family interviews, while Jolley and Maitra (in press) describe the value of a child and adolescent psychiatrist attending an adult community mental health team's case discussions monthly in order to consider problems in the children of the adult patients. This led to highly appropriate referrals, regular informal contact between the teams and increased awareness in both services about the mutual influences between children's and parents' problems.

Recent reorganisation of child protection procedures in the health service (Department of Health and Welsh Office 1995) is already assisting this liaison. Each trust has been required to identify a Named Doctor and Named Nurse for child protection, whose tasks include overseeing training across the organisation. As a result, children's issues, and child protection in particular, are acquiring a higher profile and gaps in knowledge can be more readily identified. Reder (1996a, 1996b) has commented on the valuable consultative role of trusts' Named Professionals around confidentiality dilemmas posed for adult psychiatrists and psychologists when they become aware of concerns for the safety of a patient's child.

The case reports we read for this study showed a remarkable, but common, focus on mothers, with much less detail about the children's father figures. This appeared to be either because minimal attention had been paid to them during work on the case itself, or because their influence on childcare problems was believed to be less pronounced. However, there is known to be a significant association between male violence to partners and abuse of children (e.g. Wilson *et al.* 1996; Browne and Herbert 1997) and the interaction between mother and child is also a function of the relationship between the parental couple. Professionals in the child protection network always need to give equal consideration to the child's father or father substitute, including being aware of his personal history, functioning and caretaking role, as well as the nature of the couple relationship.

General practitioners – i.e. 'family doctors' – are ideally placed to integrate issues relating to different family members, since they hold knowledge about each individual. They have the potential to commission services that meet the needs of the entire family, if necessary by referring to both child and adult resources and liaising between them. As regards child protection, general practitioners have the potential to provide invaluable contributions to multi-disciplinary training events and child protection conferences.

It is our contention that professionals will be able to help individuals better if they consider wider relationships and influences in addition to individual needs. All this can be summed up in the phrase: *'think family'*.

Practice issues

- Practitioners should be aware that parental mental health problems, especially substance misuse, heighten the risk of child maltreatment.
- Children are at increased risk of abuse by a psychotic parents when incorporated into their delusional thinking.
- Liaison between adult and child services is essential so that children of parents with mental health problems can have their needs recognised and addressed.
- Parallel assessments are necessary when a parent shows evidence of mental health problems: one, of the risk to the child from the parent's behaviour; the other, of the appropriate intervention for the parent.
- Practitioners should consider the problems of individuals in the context of their family and wider relationships.

4   Unresolved conflicts

The theoretical principles which underpin our own everyday practice and help us understand the complex dynamics of families in which child maltreatment has occurred were summarised in Chapter 1. The framework recognises that personal and interpersonal conflicts, together with the meaning that one person has for another, are core aspects of relationships and we have relied on these principles to guide our study of this group of 'Part 8' Reviews.

In this chapter, we bring together a number of related phenomena that can be considered to represent unresolved conflicts of the children's caretakers. We shall describe these conflicts and illustrate them with examples from the cases. Then, we shall argue that these observations can be integrated into a model of risk that has potential practical use.

Care and control conflicts

In the *Beyond Blame* study, we proposed that the abusive behaviour of many of the parents could be understood as a manifestation of severe personal and interpersonal problems. We described two core constellations, 'care' conflicts and 'control' conflicts, in which the parents' own childhood experiences of adverse parenting left them with unresolved tensions that spilled over into their adult relationships. These were either about being cared for and caring for others, or about self-control, wishing to control others and fearing control by them.

Similar themes recurred through the 49 cases in this study. Despite our recognition that the available family histories contained significant omissions, many of the parents had clearly experienced abuse at home and placements in alternative care. Physical abuse or neglect of a parent in childhood is specifically recorded in nine cases,[6, 12, 15, 21, 31, 34, 38, 42, 44] and at least eight primary caretakers had been in the care of the local authority during their upbringing,[6, 9, 15, 20, 29, 41, 44, 48] while others had been passed around from adult to adult.[12, 21, 42] Sexual abuse occurs much more prominently in the mothers' stories than was so in our *Beyond Blame* series,[2, 12, 28, 29, 31, 34, 44] which may well be explained by a greater readiness in the 1990s to report and recognise this problem than in the previous two decades.

As they grew older, these deprived and abused children showed many difficulties achieving a sense of autonomy and independence. A tendency to return home and then oscillate between leaving again and returning once more was common. Having a first child appeared to reawaken the wishes of young mothers to receive care from their parents, since a number returned home at that point with the infant. However, their stories suggest that this longed-for care was not forthcoming, even this time around, and they left again disappointed. One typical example was a stepfather who threw the adolescent mother-to-be out of the home, wanted her to have an abortion and refused to let her bring the baby into his house.[15]

Two variations on this pattern of personal 'leaving home' conflicts were the young mothers who took into their homes other deprived and displaced adolescents[12, 39] and the two mothers who, quite unrealistically, applied to become child minders as young adults,[6, 29] as though trying to treat their own deprivation through others.

Residues of the earlier deprivation or maltreatment dominated these individuals' behaviour and relationships in adult life. In eighteen cases, there was a clear history of violent, criminal or other antisocial behaviour from at least one of the caretakers. Seven of these male caretakers had a criminal record, including one being on the run from a prison sentence for deception,[1] another with a long history of convictions for actual bodily harm and grievous bodily harm,[22] a history of borstal and prison sentences,[41] imprisonment for grievous bodily harm[44] and Schedule 1 offences.[8] Many found partners from similar backgrounds and with similar problems. Violence between partners, not only from male to female, was clearly recorded in sixteen cases. In one family in which the mother eventually drowned the child, the couple's violent arguments included threats to kill each other.[6] One mother partnered two violent men in succession and then married a man who had allegedly sexually abused a child.[8] However, there was not an absolute correlation between parental violence and the nature of the abuse that killed the child, for these eighteen cases included two deaths from ingestion of drugs[12, 20] and one fatal assault by a babysitter.[13]

Fear of being abandoned appeared to dominate many of the

relationships, sometimes disguised as mutual threats to leave one another. One couple's rows had a recurrent pattern in which she begged him not to leave her and their violence culminated in sexual intercourse.[7] There were two examples of a male partner threatening violence to the mother if she ever left him,[2, 6] seeming to demonstrate care and control conflicts simultaneously. A reverse side of this same coin is shown by the parents who recurrently shied away from intimate relationships, presumably to avoid the risk of being hurt if the other should ever leave. The 'flight' pattern of three mothers, who moved repeatedly from home to home so that their whereabouts were unknown, can be seen as a manifestation of care and control conflicts.[1, 20, 32] In one of these cases, the child's mother had been looked after by the local authority from the age of thirteen years as beyond control and, in the final months of the child's life, moved home repeatedly between 'drug squats' and a caravan.[20]

Once parents from such backgrounds conceived a child, these residual conflicts impinged on their attitudes towards the pregnancy. Failure to attend for ante-natal care, with minimal preparation for the arrival of a dependent baby, was a major theme and occurred in at least 16 cases,[1, 4, 6, 9, 12, 13, 15, 21, 26, 31, 32, 41, 42, 44, 45, 48] most usually with the pregnancy of the child who eventually died. Furthermore, it is uncommon for mothers to take overdoses of tablets during pregnancy, which could represent either a positive wish to kill the foetus as well as themselves or a denial of the life within them: it is recorded in two cases.[12, 15] One infant was born with severe drug withdrawal because of the mother's continued drug use during the pregnancy[45] and another mother is reported to have drunk liberally during the pregnancy.[15]

Absence of post-natal care also featured significantly,[1, 4, 11, 26, 32, 41, 48] including refusal to attend clinics or admit health visitors for developmental checks. We inferred that this represented an inability to prioritise the infant's needs for care and we were particularly struck by the number of mothers who inappropriately tried to wean their babies on to solids when only a few weeks old, as though wishing them to be older than they were .[2, 13, 15, 31, 46] One mother told her social worker that she sometimes thought of her baby, then just a few weeks of age, as two or three years old, although she knew that this was inappropriate.[21]

Frustration with children's normal infantile behaviour was more difficult to discover from the chronologies, although one father is reported to have resented the baby's crying[41] and a mother slapped her baby for urinating whilst she was changing the nappy.[31] Information about the moments leading up to the fatal assault were only recorded in four of the files, but they suggest that intolerance of an infant's uncontrollable behaviour is crucial. One mother wanted to give up breast-feeding her two-week-old baby and gave her a bottle when she woke in the night: she strangled her when she continued to be grizzly. Another mother snapped when her nine-week-old child cried and tried to pull her hair.[21] One mother's cohabitee fatally assaulted the ten-month-old child, who had soiled and urinated in the bath,[7] while a father reached the end of his tether because of his four-month-old infant's inconsolable crying.[15]

There was little evidence in these cases of the complete closing off from all contact with professionals that we observed in many of the *Beyond Blame* cases, perhaps because prolonged professional involvement was not such a feature. However, there were a number of examples of parents refusing to admit a health visitor, lying that the mother and child were not at home or refusing to attend appointments. One father, who drank heavily and used drugs, was repeatedly hostile and intimidating to professionals who visited.[17] A few parents showed 'disguised compliance', apparently agreeing to professionals' requirements of them but then failing to carry them out. Another father aggressively refused entry to the health visitor one day but, fearing increased surveillance by statutory agencies, visited the health centre the next day to make an appointment.[28]

In summary, we are proposing that care conflicts arose out of actual experiences of abandonment, neglect or rejection as a child, or feeling unloved by parents. They showed in later life as: excessive reliance on others and fear of being left by them; or, its counterpart, distancing themselves from others; intolerance of a partner's or child's dependency; unwillingness to prepare antenatally for an infant's dependency needs; or declining to respond to the needs when the child was born. Control conflicts were based on childhood experiences of feeling helpless in the face of sexual or physical abuse or neglect, or inappropriate limit-setting. In adult life, they were enacted through: violence; low frustration tolerance; suspiciousness; threats of violence; or other attempts to assert power over others. Violence or control issues could become part of their relationships with partners, children, professionals or society in general.

Often, parents showed evidence of both types of conflicts in their relationships with others. Criminal behaviour such as stealing, for example, could result from experiences of both deprivation and violence in childhood. Similarly, substance misuse, which often has its origins in earlier deprivation, substitutes dependency on drugs or alcohol for absent care and results in episodes of out-of-control behaviour.

The following case vignettes illustrate how constellations of these conflicts ran through the unhappy lives of the families.

As a 16-year-old, the child's mother had left home, become pregnant unintentionally, sought minimal antenatal and post-natal care and returned to her own mother's home with her 10-month-old infant. However, this young mother's own mother was herself pregnant again and was more preoccupied with her own needs than those of her daughter. The 16-year-old's baby then appeared to become caught in the middle of her attempts to receive care for herself, for when the grandmother did show an interest in the baby, the mother abandoned her. She then reclaimed the baby, possibly with the intention of using her as a reason to meet the child's father again. Once again, when the father did show an interest in his child, the mother left them, too. Thereafter, she showed a pattern of flight, moving from home to home, until living with the man who killed her child.[1]

We understand this young woman to have shown unresolved dependency through her 'leaving home' dilemma, early pregnancy, failure to prioritise the baby's needs and using the child in an attempt to secure care for herself.

One mother's mother had abandoned her to be brought up by her grandmother until she was 18 months old and, once she had returned, the stepfather physically and sexually abused her. She was looked after by the local authority when aged 14 and her first child was unwanted and born two days after her grandmother had died. She had had minimal antenatal care and started the baby on solids when just 2 months old. She recurrently went out drinking, leaving the child with her own mother or other unsuitable caretakers, which included deprived and displaced young adolescents whom she took into her home. The child suffered chronic neglect and died from ingestion of drugs.[12]

We infer that this mother's unresolved care conflicts impacted significantly on her ability to meet the dependency needs of her young baby.

The following example illustrates caretakers' behaviour seemingly dominated by the need to control others.

The child's mother was probably sexually abused in childhood by her father. As an adult, she repeatedly kept professionals 'at bay' by agreeing to register with a GP, to attend review meetings and take the child to hospital, but always failed to do so. Her apparent compliance undermined professionals' attempts to confront her with ultimatums. A violent cohabitee threatened that if she ever left him, he would come looking for her. It was he who fatally assaulted the child.[2]

A combination of unresolved care and control conflicts were apparent in many families, as exemplified below.

A mother, who came from an army family, was said to share her father's negative attitude to social workers and to be scared of authority. She repeatedly missed hospital appointments for the child's chronic illness and ignored his needs. Her neglectful parenting increased when her partner left her whilst she was pregnant again, after which she tried to move back to be near her own parents again. The child's death from his medical condition was undoubtedly hastened by neglect.[39]

Overall, then, we saw a recurrent theme running through many of the cases in which the parents showed some constellation of unresolved care and/or control conflicts. They had their origins in childhood and were played out in behaviour and relationships in adult life. These observations are supported by a number of reports in the literature about parents who abuse that can be translated into this framework. Green *et al.* (1974) described mothers who found that their child's nurturant demands intensified their own unsatisfied dependency feelings and who instead relied on the child to satisfy these unmet needs. They also showed poor self-concept and poor impulse control. Pianta *et al.* (1989: 207) inferred from more recent research findings on abusing mothers that:

Women who have not resolved interpersonal issues of trust, dependency, and autonomy are likely to be considerably stressed when faced with the demands of a highly dependent child ... They may also find themselves seeking to meet their own emotional needs in the context of the parent–child relationship and may experience hostility toward the child when those needs are not met.

Parents who induce illnesses in their children – the Munchausen syndrome-by-proxy – have also been described as coming from emotionally deprived backgrounds and pursuing a compulsion to control and defeat medical staff (e.g. Gray and Bentovim 1996; Loader and Kelly 1996).

Tuteur and Glotzer (1966) noted that all of the 'murdering' mothers they interviewed had grown up in emotionally cold and rejecting environments and usually showed extreme dependency needs which they carried into their marriage union and which were seldom satisfactorily met. In her study of fatal abuse cases, Wilczynski (1997) found that 44 per cent of the child homicide suspects studied had suffered maltreatment or disruption in childhood, including having been made the subject of a Care Order, experienced abuse or neglect, witnessed significant parental conflict or violence, or been separated from a parent before the age of fifteen years.

Crimmins *et al.* (1997) coined the term 'motherless mothers' for many of the convicted women murderers they studied. The women's mothers had been unavailable to them emotionally or had been absent during their childhood, had subjected them to prolonged abuse and/or had suffered from alcoholism and other mental health problems. The majority of the women who had killed their children had such histories and had also been involved with an abusive partner. Their self-perceptions were considered to be so damaged that they believed abuse was all they deserved. Many had also abused drugs or alcohol themselves in adult life.

An association between child abuse and deficient perinatal care is only occasionally referred to in the literature. Polansky *et al.* (1981) found subsequent child neglect significantly higher from mothers who had waited more than three months before registering their pregnancy with a doctor, while refusal to attend, or dropping out of, prenatal classes was associated with subsequent child abuse in Egan *et al.*'s prospective study (1990). Inadequate prenatal care was included in the risk factors collated by Stewart and Gangbar (1984), Benedict *et al.* (1985), Anderson (1987) and Schloesser *et al.* (1992). Intra-uterine exposure of the foetus to drugs by substance-misusing mothers was found to be linked to later maltreatment of the child by Kelley (1992) and Jaudes *et al.* (1995). An incidental finding of Ounsted *et al.*'s study (1982) of pregnant mothers considered 'at risk' was that later evidence of child abuse occurred mainly in those families who could not be included in the study because they had discharged themselves prematurely from the post-natal ward.

Krugman (1985) found clear triggers in 19 of 24 cases of fatal abuse. Nine of the children had been assaulted following a toileting accident or messy nappy change and seven after inconsolable crying. Scott (1973) considered that there was always an immediately precipitating stimulus from the child, such as vomiting, screaming or food refusal, which the fathers he studied had interpreted as defiance or rejection and Korbin (1987) also reports that perceptions of rejection underlay fatal assaults following the child's crying or food refusal. Brewster *et al.* (1998) reviewed 32 infant maltreatment deaths and found that the victim's crying precipitated the fatal assault in 58 per cent of cases.

Our description of care and control dynamics correlates with other psychologies for understanding human relationships and, in particular, with Bowlby's attachment theory (e.g. Bowlby 1969, 1973, 1980, 1977, 1988; Ainsworth 1982; Holmes 1993; Heard and Lake 1997). In essence, Bowlby described an innate dynamic between infant and parent in which the infant sought attachment upon and proximity to reliable parent figures and the parents provided the infant with a secure base from which to explore the world. Sensitive parental care helped the child develop self-reliance and self-esteem, as well as confidence that other people could be relied upon when needed and a readiness to cooperate with them. Conversely, rejection of the child's attachment overtures could result in anxiety, overdependency (although Bowlby did not like the term 'dependency') or avoidance of proximity and lack of concern for others.

Bowlby linked care-seeking behaviour with anger so that, within the evolving attachment dynamic, anxiety and anger were considered natural responses to the risk of loss and that 'a great deal of maladaptive violence met with in families can be understood as the distorted and exaggerated versions of behaviour that is potentially functional, especially attachment behaviour on the one hand and caregiving behaviour on the other' (1988: 81). Bowlby addressed himself to child abuse and described abusive parents as typically showing the extreme characteristics of anxious attachment in which they yearned for care but expected only rejection. These feelings were based on childhood experiences of rejection, unreliable or hostile parenting or threats of abandonment (1988).

> Small wonder, therefore, if when a woman with this background becomes a mother, that there are times when, instead of being ready to mother her child, she looks to the child to mother her. Small wonder too if when her child fails to oblige and starts crying, demanding care and attention, that she gets angry and impatient with it.
>
> (Bowlby 1988: 86)

Violent men were also described as showing the consequences of earlier ill-treatment and rejection, including jealousy at the attention their partner showed to a baby and coercive attempts to control, even 'imprison', their partner. Bowlby considered that such anxiously attached men commonly ended up in partnerships with equally anxiously attached women and they would enact recurrent cycles of proximity-seeking followed by aggressive distancing behaviour between them.

The tendency for childhood attachment experiences to be recapitulated in relationships in later life is encapsulated in Bowlby's concept of 'internal working models'. These are considered to be assumptions, or generalisations, about self and others that the child builds up, based on repeated patterns of interactive experiences, which form representational models that are used to predict and relate to the world (Holmes 1993).

Heard and Lake (1997) are among those who have developed Bowlby's ideas. They discuss how a common consequence of disrupted attachment in childhood is relating through dominating or submissive forms in adult life, typified by those who force others to follow the controlling leader. During childhood, such people cannot trust caregivers to be interested in their plight or to treat them with respect. In adult life, they feel incompetent and powerless when faced with too many careseekers or ones that are uncooperative. In order to regain a sense of control and competence, they fall back on coercively controlling or avoidant patterns of relating, especially when currently experiencing threatened or actual loss of a caretaker or sense of competence.

In our view, the care–control conflicts model has a number of implications. The frequency with which absent antenatal and post-natal care occurred in these cases points toward a period when risk assessments and preventive measures might usefully be targeted. It seems that perinatal assessment of parents' attitudes towards the pregnancy should be considered if antenatal care has been minimal and the young parent is from a deprived background. Although the average age at which the parents in this series started to bear children was not particularly young, the idea of unresolved care conflicts can help make sense of the observation that some did become parents in mid or late teens. We would suggest that it is the meaning for that parent of having a child so young that is important and whether, for instance, it is intended to reverse a sense of personal deprivation, or in the hope that the child will provide them with the love that they missed earlier in their lives.

The meaning of the child

We shall now consider in greater detail how unresolved conflicts can influence the meaning that a child has for its caretakers. We introduced the notion of the meaning of the child in *Beyond Blame* when we inferred that some children in the households had been at greater risk of harm than others because they carried a particular psychological significance for their caretaker(s). It was as though the children acquired an undeclared script or blueprint for their life that submerged their personal identity and characteristics and this meaning came to dominate the parent–child relationship. In the words of Ron Britton (personal communication), the children became 'actors in someone else's play'.

We suggested that children may acquire particular meanings through, for example: being born at the same time as a transitional event in the parent's life and thereafter always being associated with its emotional sequelae; having certain physical or personality characteristics; being unwanted; being expected to fulfil a role in the parent's life that was associated with the parent's unresolved conflicts; and so on. The meaning of the child includes the parent's overt and covert motivations for wanting and having a child, as well as conscious and unconscious determinants of the parent's attitudes to, feelings about and relationship with the particular child (Reder and Duncan 1995b).

We noted similar phenomena in the present study and were struck that opportunities for considering the meaning of a child, and therefore whether that child might be at risk of maltreatment, arose during the antenatal period as well as during the child's later life. For instance, a number of mothers admitted that their pregnancy had been unwanted and that the child, once born, continued to be unwanted.[6, 12] Sometimes this was made explicit through requests for the child to be adopted or manifest ambivalence about keeping the baby.

One mother denied her unplanned pregnancy and received no antenatal care until three months before the birth. She wanted to terminate the pregnancy but this was opposed by the father and their disagreement was the cause of continuing conflict between them. The mother had been emotionally dependent on her parents and the child's father whilst they were together. However, the pregnancy coincided with the maternal grandfather's death and the couple then separated when the child was eight months of age. Two months after this, the mother asked for him to be adopted. She admitted to her GP that he had been looked after by others for most of his life and volunteered to the social worker that he was a reminder to her of his absent father. However, four days after signing the adoption papers, she took him back and wanted to have a joint meeting with the father. She continued to place the infant in the care of others and told her family aide that she wished the child had never been born. The baby was killed by her cohabitee when aged 17 months.[1]

We suggest that the mother's ambivalence was based on her perception that the child competed with her for fulfilment of dependency wishes. The child seemed to be associated in her mind with the loss of her own father, and then her partner, and she may even have believed that the child had the capacity to cause separations and reconciliations. There was no information available to enable us to speculate on the meaning of the child for the mother's cohabitee in this, or the following, case.

The child was believed to be the result of incestuous abuse by the mother's father. After her birth, the mother oscillated between leaving her parental home and returning again, sometimes leaving the child in the grandmother's care. The child was frequently neglected and seen to be bruised and finally killed by the mother's cohabitee.[2]

This child appeared to us to carry multiple meanings to her mother, including being the living evidence of her sexual abuse and being caught up in her conflict about leaving home and becoming independent of her own mother. Opportunities had occurred in the antenatal period to inquire about the child's psychological heritage, since the mother was just 19 years old and unmarried.

During childhood, another mother had been brought up by her grandmother because of her own mother's lack of interest. When she did return to her mother's home, her stepfather physically and sexually abused her and she was made the subject of a Care Order as being beyond parental control. When she, in turn, became a mother, she would not contemplate respite care for her infant because her own mother might find out, even though she frequently left the child alone or with unsuitable caretakers or threatened to abandon him. The child suffered persistent neglect and died from ingesting medicines.[12]

It occurred to us that the child's role was to prove that the mother could be a better parent than her own mother had been to her but was also experienced as a rival for receipt of care.

The delivery of the first child of one mother was traumatic as she believed that she could have died from a haemorrhage. In addition, her previously well-controlled epilepsy returned after the birth. The obstetrician agreed to deliver any future children by Caesarean section. Within a few weeks, the mother developed hallucinations and threatened violence to her husband and the baby, whom she said that she hated. Two years later, she was anxious to become pregnant again but, four years after that, decided to have a termination rather than expose herself to the risk of childbirth. She then wished to adopt but the couple were turned down after assessment. Three years later, when the mother was aged 40, she told her GP that she wanted another baby but only if born by Caesarean section. Within three weeks of that child's birth, the mother told her midwife that she hated the baby and told her husband that the baby might be dead before he returned home from his night shift. She eventually smothered the child.[3]

Here, it is the meaning of children in general to the mother that seems significant, since she appears to have perceived them as extremely damaging to her, even though wanted.

The importance of the perinatal period for considering the meaning of the child is supported by other authors. Roberts (1988) characterises children's vulnerability to abuse as being related to whether they were born too soon, born sick or handicapped, born different, or born unwanted. Subsequent abuse of the child has been found to be associated with mothers who considered abortion (Hunter *et al.* 1978; Egan *et al.* 1990), who did not accept their pregnancy (Vietze *et al.* 1991) or whose pregnancy was unplanned and unwanted (Altemeier *et al.* 1984; Murphy *et al.* 1985). Korbin (1986) discusses a series of mothers who had killed their children: one recalled her own parents' disappointment that she was female and then her own later extreme anxiety when she began to bathe her male baby. Another mother had been sadistically sexually abused by her stepfather and she believed that stepchildren were in particular jeopardy: she fiercely protected her son from his stepfather, but allowed their biological child to die of starvation.

Such examples from the literature and from our two studies concentrate on the meanings of children for mothers. Most of the case files in this present study did not contain sufficient detail about the male caretakers to enable us to hypothesise about psychological meanings of the child for them. Clearly, it is equally relevant to understand the meaning for men of caring for children in the light of their own background and personal relationships and for non-biological fathers of caring for a child from the mother's previous liaison. For example, cohabitees or stepfathers may be jealous of the mother's previous intimacy with another man and experience the child as a constant reminder of this. The child may also be experienced as a 'stranger', competing with him for the mother's affection and giving him nothing emotionally in return (Wilson and Daly 1987). Future studies and reports would be helped if authors clarified the status of the caretaking couple's relationship and whether a non-biological partner is the mother's husband, a long-standing cohabitee or a temporary liaison.

Towards a model of risk

Assessment of risk in child protection work is not easy and guidance has tended to be offered in the form of high-risk checklists (e.g. Greenland 1987). We have discussed previously (Reder *et al.* 1993a) the limitations of attributional checklists, which may inhibit professionals' thinking rather than enhance it. They tend not to provide enough information that is specific to the dynamics of the case in question, since it is the *meaning* of individual attributes in the context of interpersonal functioning that gives more valid clues to the risk. Our approach is therefore inclined towards process factors, and this study has suggested to us a simplified interactional model of risk that might have general application.

The model starts with the commonly agreed scheme for under-standing physical abuse of children, which was discussed in Chapter 1 but is worth reprising here:

> abusing parents ... tend to be lonely, unhappy, angry adults under heavy stress. They injure their children after being provoked by some misbehaviour, and often themselves have experienced phys-ical abuse as children ... The child often has characteristics that make him or her provocative, such as negativism or a difficult temperament; some of the more offensive misbehaviours are intractable crying, wetting, soiling, and spilling. The occasion initiating the abuse is usually a family crisis; the most common crises include loss of a job or home, marital strife or upheavals, birth of a sibling, or physical exhaustion.
>
> (Schmitt and Krugman 1992: 79)

This summary helps us construct a model of abusive circumstances in which there is an interrelationship between parents with unresolved personal conflicts, vulnerable children and social stress, as in Figure 4.1.

Both the *Beyond Blame* study and this present review have enabled us to add further detail to this picture. Most abusing parents can be described as suffering from unresolved care and control conflicts; the children are especially at risk during the early months and years, when they are most dependent and when they carry meanings for their parent(s) associated with the unresolved parental conflicts. The fami-lies live in stressful circumstances, including conditions of social stress and relationship disharmony. Even when the maltreatment is of long-standing duration, there appear to be episodes of increased stress which precipitate escalation of abuse.

It was possible to infer from the cases in both of our studies some common patterns to the situations that led to increased abuse. These can then be built on to the model of abuse described above to generate a model of risk. The risk factors can be considered as either crises in the parents' relationships with their social context or crises in the parents' interactions with their children. More particularly, the crises are additional stresses to the parents' already conflictual caring or controlling relationships.

For example, in this present study, we found that parents were more liable to abuse when they felt rejected or abandoned, most commonly by their own parents or by a partner. This might have come about through actual separation, emotional distancing or simply the threat of

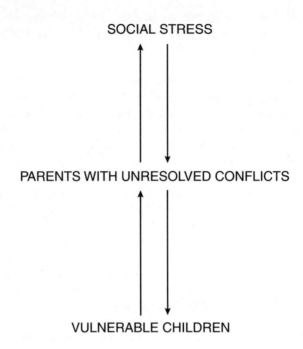

Figure 4.1   A model of child abuse

being left. For some, a similar reaction followed the withdrawal of supportive services by professionals or loss of housing. In others, the death of a person who once looked after them, even if that care had been hostile, seemed to reawaken dormant conflicts about unfulfilled wishes for care. Equivalent problems arose if the parent had left their family of origin but returned home again, as though hoping to receive at this later stage the care that they had previously missed, only to discover that their relationship with their parent(s) had not changed. Insults to an already impoverished self-esteem, such as when failing to achieve a longed-for goal, also added to the stress. For example, one mother killed her child a few months after her claim for compensation for the sexual abuse that she had suffered from her father was turned down.[31]

Escalation in an abusing couple's rows appeared to threaten both care and control conflicts by raising the prospects of abandonment or of uncontrolled violence. Mounting violence between a couple, accompanied by increasing substance misuse, seemed particularly dangerous for the same reasons. As we discussed in *Beyond Blame*, when professionals put extra pressure on parents to cooperate, or demonstrably increase their monitoring activities, this often exaggerates parents' fear of being controlled.

We infer from this review that parent–child interactions were stressed by increases in dependency demands upon the parents, such as when a mother realised she was pregnant again or when she gave birth to a baby. Refusing antenatal and post-natal care, or ignoring the baby's basic needs, seemed to represent a wish to deny the extra dependency demands. Other episodes of added stress came when a child, or another member of the family, became ill, and most especially if the child temporarily regressed. It seems likely that moment-to-moment care crises occurred when the child cried persistently or demanded attention in other ways, such as by soiling a nappy. In addition, these episodes exaggerated control conflicts, since the parent was liable to experience the child's demands for care as controlling of them. We presume that the tension increased further when the child was not pacified by the parent's comforting attempts, since this would have been experienced as rejection. A child whose dependency needs curtailed the parent's freedom was probably also perceived as controlling.

We are proposing, therefore, that in many of the cases, the risk of increasing abuse to the child was linked to crises in their caretakers' unresolved care and/or control conflicts. An escalating scenario developed in which stresses to the parental care–control conflicts came together over days and weeks and built up until one final precipitating incident resulted in the fatal assault.

In addition, we would suggest that a related constellation of stressors further increased the risk to some children. These were crises in the meaning of the child for their caretaker. We have already discussed how some children were probably born with expectations that they could solve a parent's care conflicts. The parent might have hoped that the child would provide them with the affection that they felt was missing from their family of origin, or be the means of resuming a relationship with a separated partner or parent. It is likely that crises occurred when the child failed in this allotted task, so that they were punished or became the target of their parents' frustrations. Other children seemed linked in their parents' minds with uncomfortable feelings associated with major life events, such as a death or separation, especially if the child's birth coincided with that event. Children who were conceived through incestuous abuse were the ever-present reminder to the mother of her experiences.

Presumably, the conflict associated with these meanings reached a crisis when the parent was acutely reminded of the child's significance for them and that the child was failing to fulfil its ascribed task. In particular, when the child's meaning arose out of the parent's unresolved care and/or control conflicts, crises in the parental conflicts created a crisis in the child's meaning. In other words, an escalating vicious circle developed with reverberations between the child's meaning and the parent's current emotional crisis. The nature of the child's meaning fuelled the crisis for the parent and this precipitated abuse.

To elaborate further, a hypothetical example would be if the partner abandoned an emotionally deprived mother who had wished that her child would provide her with the love she had never received during her childhood. Another scenario might be a stepchild, living with a mother and non-biological father whose marriage was dominated by mutual fears of abandonment. The child would have become a continual reminder to the non-biological parent that his partner once had an intimate relationship with another man. Should the child overtly defy his authority or covertly challenge his status in the family, he would be acutely reminded of his insecurity. Again, an unwanted child of an emotionally deprived mother is likely to be rejected or neglected continuously, but a crisis would occur during an event which placed extra demands on the mother to be caring, such as an illness in the child or a further pregnancy.

We can use this model to explain another specific risk factor which we have noted in this study and which has been reported by others. It is clear that a child is in significant danger from a parent suffering from a psychotic illness if they have been incorporated into the parent's delusional thinking. For example, the parent may speak to the child as though they were someone else, or they may hear hallucinations with messages about the child. Translated into our model, a crisis has occurred in the meaning of the child because the child has taken on a new meaning to the parent, albeit one based on delusional thinking.

The notion of crises in care or control relationships or in the meaning of the child can be incorporated into the model of abuse from Figure 4.1 to produce a model of risk, as depicted in Figure 4.2.

This is a simplified model and may not account for all circumstances of severe abuse. However, we would suggest that it does encompass many of the risk factors identified through this study and in the previous *Beyond Blame* project. It also helps give meaning to many of the high risk factors reported in the literature, as indicated in Table 4.1. This table contains a representative group of risk factors

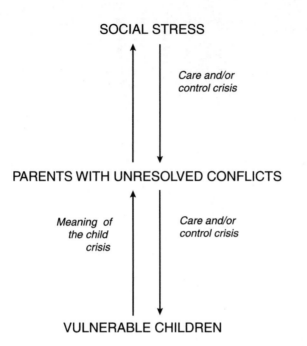

Figure 4.2 A model of risk of child abuse

from the literature, alongside which we have given our own interpretations of the factors within the model of care–control and meaning of the child conflicts. The table is not intended as an assessment checklist but as a summary of risk factors previously reported in the literature which can be translated into our framework and support our proposed model of risk.

Parental unresolved conflicts would seem to be significant factors to be assessed in child protection cases. In the next chapter, we shall discuss how problems with the assessment process itself were a prominent feature of the cases reviewed in this study.

Table 4.1 Examples of child abuse risk factors translated into 'care/control' and 'meaning of the child' conflicts

Risk Factor	Hunter et al. 1978 (prospective study of newborn)	Greenland 1987 (review of fatal abuse cases)	Browne and Saqi 1988 (study of predictive values)	Whipple and Webster-Stratton 1991 (study of stress factors)	Presumed unresolved conflict
Parental history of abuse or neglect	+	+	+	+	Care and/or control
Impulsive, apathetic or dependent personality	+				Care
Young mother	+		+	+	Care
Retarded parent or inadequate education	+			+	
Fractured family, including:					
marital disharmony or violence	+		+	+	Care and/or control
separations, single, non-biological parent	+	+	+	+	Care/meaning of child
History of maltreating a child	+	+			Care and/or control
Inadequate child spacing	+				Care
Poor use of medical care	+				Care and/or control
Inadequate childcare arrangements	+				Care
Socially isolated	+	+		+	Care and/or control
Financial difficulties, poverty, unemployment	+	+	+	+	Care and/or control
Alcohol/drug misuse		+		+	Control
History of violence/criminality		+			Care
History of suicide attempts/mental illness		+	+		Care
Pregnant or post-partum		+			Meaning of child
Unwanted child, incl. considered abortion	+				Meaning of child
Disappointed over sex of child	+				Care
Child young		+			
Child health problems, including:					
premature, low birth weight, perinatal separation		+	+		Care/Meaning of child
birth defect or disability		+			Meaning of child
feeding or elimination difficulties		+			Care and/or control
Child difficult to comfort					Care and/or control
Indifference, intolerance or overanxiety to child			+		Care

Practice issues

- Practitioners should look for evidence of unresolved care and/or control conflicts in parents who abuse their children.
- Parents may imbue children with particular psychological meanings which render them more vulnerable to maltreatment and this should be included in assessments of risk.
- The perinatal period provides an ideal opportunity for professionals to assess parental unresolved conflicts and the meaning of the child, as a means of targeting preventive strategies.
- Evidence of ambivalence to motherhood, such as changing wishes about whether to give up a newborn child for adoption, should be explored further with the parent(s) before a final decision is made.
- The notion of crises in unresolved conflicts can help professionals assess risk of significant harm to children.

5   Assessments

One practice issue stood out above all others in this review and was repeated in case after case. It concerned problems with assessment. In this chapter, we shall first describe and illustrate the assessment problems that we identified. Then, we shall consider some of the core principles underlying assessment in order to discuss how approaches to assessment might be improved.

In the cases reviewed, we identified the following types of problems with assessments: (a) dissonance between assessment and action; (b) assessments not undertaken; (c) thresholds of concern not reached; (d) warnings unrecognised; and (e) assessment paralysis. We have already discussed assessment paralysis in Chapter 3 (see page 56) and here we shall focus on the other four concerns.

Dissonance between assessment and action

While assessments were undertaken in some cases, problems arose in following through their implications into appropriate interventions. The need for assessment was recognised and relevant information was sought but the findings failed to guide subsequent action. In one case, this occurred at least twice.

The mother was referred for psychiatric treatment following conviction for the murder of her first child. The staff who treated her were not fully convinced of her culpability and her psychiatrist appeared to consider her more as a victim of physical and sexual abuse in childhood than as a murderer. When the mother became pregnant again, her psychiatrist's court report highlighted many unresolved care–control conflicts that we would regard as indicative of significant risk of future abuse, but her final recommendations supported the mother assuming care of her baby. Social workers compiled a list of risk factors from their own assessment and decided to recommend that the mother should not care for the baby. However, additional psychiatric reports to the court gave contrary opinions and, instead of retaining confidence in their own judgements, social services backed down and agreed to a plan to support the mother–child relationship. Social workers' reports to subsequent hearings focused on positive points and emphasised evidence of good bonding, rather than the mother's vulnerability to being left by her partner, which they had previously clearly identified as likely to precipitate her into outbursts of frustrated violence. She ultimately also smothered her second child.[31]

Ironically, this was one of only two cases in which there had been full court hearings to consider a child's future care – circumstances which one might expect to facilitate coherence between assessments and actions. However, two influences that we have discussed in *Beyond Blame* seemed to skew the plan of action. First, the psychiatrist appeared to hold a 'pervasive belief' that the mother was primarily a victim rather than culpable of infanticide. Second, an 'exaggeration of hierarchy' in the professional network meant that the social workers backed down from the clear conclusions of their own assessment.

When setting out to monitor child protection plans, it is essential to have clarified from the outset what observations would lead practitioners to infer that the plan was continuing successfully or, on the other hand, failing. Professionals given the task of monitoring the plan must be made aware of the problem, the plan and the criteria. In some of the cases reviewed, assessments were undertaken and child protection plans made, but no criteria were identified for what would constitute success or failure of the plan.

In one instance, staff of a special care baby unit were left to monitor a mother's early parenting because a family centre could not admit them. However, they were not made fully aware of the nature of the concerns or the factors to be observed. They told the social worker that the mother's visits 'went well' and the child was therefore allowed home, only to be killed by his mother when aged 5 weeks.[21]

Because the observations were being made in a medical setting rather than one specialising in child protection, we would consider it even more important to have specified the criteria by which to judge the potential for significant harm. This is also an example of the phenomenon of 'role confusion' that we have described in *Beyond Blame*, in which the tasks appropriate to one profession were assigned to others who had neither the skills nor responsibilities to carry them out.

> Another mother, who had severe drug dependency problems and two previous failed attempts at detoxification, entered a drug rehabilitation unit with her infant as a 'final chance'. She was informed that the rules of the unit included discharge if she were found to be taking drugs whilst a resident. Although her urine samples repeatedly showed that she was continuing to take alcohol and drugs, the treatment was not deemed to have failed and the child returned home with the mother. The child died at 10 weeks of age and, although the death was recorded as SIDS, we remain suspicious that neglect contributed significantly.[45]

Here, previously agreed consequences were not invoked despite obvious evidence of the failure criteria and, when the mother defaulted from the programme, no one translated this into the need to undertake a parenting reassessment and to revise the child protection plan.

Assessments not undertaken

The most common assessment problem in the cases reviewed was that assessments were not undertaken following notification of a child maltreatment concern. Sometimes, this meant that a referral received no specific response at all or that minimal information was sought from unreliable sources.

> In one case, a duty social worker telephoned the mother's land-lady following an anonymous allegation of abuse and was satisfied when she replied that she was not concerned.[32]

Alternatively, interventions were planned and decisions taken but they did not appear to have been guided by any assessment. We wondered whether this might have been due to omissions by the reviewers when compiling the chronologies, so that assessments had been performed but were simply not recorded. However, there were so many examples of this absence of reported assessments that we believe a more likely explanation is that they were, indeed, not performed. Three cases will serve as examples of the many.

A mother changed her mind about placing her baby for adoption four days after she had signed the adoption papers. The child was returned to her care without any apparent assessment of her relationship with, and attitude to, the child. In this same case, parental responsibility and contact were agreed outside the court without the benefit of an assessment, just eleven days before the mother's cohabitee killed the child.[1]

As with numerous other cases in the study, minimal information was recorded in this review report about either caretaker's background, so that we were unable to make much sense of their emotional or relationship functioning or of the meaning of the child to them. We presume that the relevant information, and therefore this understanding, was not available to the workers at the time.

Another child was returned home to his parents without any assessment of the home circumstances, even though he had run off and said he was afraid to return there.[38]

When a child runs away from home and expresses such fears, current abuse within the home should be high in practitioners' thinking and therefore needs to be assessed.

A general practitioner told a child protection conference that he would not be surprised if an infant's mother had inflicted the burns on him but he considered it unlikely that she would do it again. The case file does not record any assessment which informed this opinion. That same conference had recommended further social work and psychiatric assessment but they were never done.[28]

There were other cases in which the need for an assessment was recognised and decisions made to undertake one. However, the chronology then went on to describe an intervention without any mention that the assessment had been attempted or, if one was done, there was a failure to record the outcome and conclusions of any assessment.

Occasionally, some form of assessment was undertaken but we would suggest that it missed pertinent issues.

> A mother applied for her 10-month-old infant to be returned to her care from the grandmother's, under a Residence Order. The judge asked for a social work assessment of the suitability of the home. This assessment focused mainly on material factors, such as the suitability of the accommodation, which was a rented caravan, as well as whether the mother's cohabitee was known to the police and whether the mother would allow continued contact with the grandmother.[2]

In *Beyond Blame*, we coined the term 'concrete solutions' for practitioners' tendency to concentrate on material factors when considering the potential safety of children. While they are undoubtedly relevant, it is essential also to address the psychological and relationship issues in the family. In our reading of this case, the assessment also needed to include the origins of the continuing conflict between the mother and grandmother, especially in view of an allegation that the child had been conceived through incestuous abuse. More light might then have been shed on the meaning of the child to the mother and her choice of partners. Furthermore, there was inadequate assessment of the cohabitee's potential as a parental figure and it was he who killed the child two months later.

> In another case, long-standing concerns about a child who was living with her mother whilst she suffered from psychotic delusions culminated in social services referring the child for an assessment. She was referred for this assessment to a paediatrician, who concentrated on reviewing her physical development.[6]

For us, concern should have included the emotional well-being and physical safety of the child, so that mental health assessments of the child and of the mother's parenting would have been appropriate.

Thresholds of concern not reached

We had noted in *Beyond Blame* a tendency for professionals to treat information discretely and not to consider fresh developments in the context of what was already known about the family. As a result, many new alerts about children's safety were dealt with in isolation and, consequently, thresholds of concern were not reached. Very different pictures might have emerged if the latest events had been integrated with the catalogue of previous problems, so that awareness of risk heightened with accumulated knowledge. In this way, concerns could have reached a critical threshold which, in turn, could have determined that a different professional response was needed.

Two concepts from other domains of thinking could provide further understanding of this. The first has its origins in the 'gestalt' principle, which argues that the whole is greater than the sum of its parts. Each element only gives a partial picture but, taken together, a new meaning emerges at a different level of understanding. The other idea is contained in the distinction made between first- and second-order change (Watzlawick *et al.* 1974). The analogy is often given of the kaleidoscope, in which small turns of the eyepiece produce minor shifts in pattern of the crystals viewed (a first-order change). Eventually, however, one further small turn precipitates a massive reorganisation of their relative positions and a totally new pattern (a second-order change). Thus, in assessments, putting newly acquired information into the context of that which is already known can allow a comparatively small change in total information to precipitate a major transformation in thought and action.

While conducting this present study, we often paused from reading a chronology when our retrospective anxiety for the child had been raised by a new piece of information. We then listed out the main elements of the case that, taken together, indicated to us that a threshold of risk of significant harm had been reached. Three examples will serve as illustrations.

A mother had been abandoned as a baby by her own mother, had been physically, and possibly sexually, abused by her step-father and had been taken into the care of the local authority as a teenager as being beyond parental control. She had been suspended from school for sniffing glue and drinking and, as an adult, abused alcohol and drugs. She and her husband frequently left their children at home alone while they were out drinking. During the pregnancy of the child who died, the mother had had minimal antenatal care and had taken an overdose of tablets. She volunteered to her social worker that she had considered putting the baby up for adoption and later 'felt sick of' the infant but had 'now got over it'. Both children of this mother were neglected and the child who died was frequently left in the care of different people. New alerts included reports of rough handling, burn marks, unsuitable babysitters, the children playing unsupervised, the children returning home alone from school, the children knocking on neighbours' doors asking for food, parental drinking, and the elder sister approaching strangers and expressing fears of going home. One child protection conference was called during six years of intermittent professional involvement with the family, after the police had found the children unattended at home, but social services closed the case within a month. Previously, at the birth of the mother's first child, a social worker observed her rough handling of the baby and aggression towards ward staff but decided there were insufficient grounds for a child protection conference. Two years later, a social worker responded to the grandmother's concerns about the mother's parenting by saying a conference could be called if there were sufficient concerns. The integrated chronology catalogues persistent neglect and physical abuse by the parents and evidence of significant harm to the elder child. Yet a planning meeting, held just two months before the younger child died from ingestion of drugs, agreed that, although there were some parenting concerns, there had been improvements.[12]

This mother's childhood history contained much evidence of unresolved care and control conflicts and her adult lifestyle implied continued impact of these problems. Each new element of the evolving story was further evidence for us of the mother's ambivalence to her children and inability to meet their dependency needs and that the harm they were suffering was mounting. With each new alert, we inferred that there already was sufficient knowledge of risk to the children to have required protective measures. However, it had not been collated together as summarised here, so that specific information did not acquire new meaning.

> In another case, a health visitor referred the family to social services after the mother, who suffered from paranoid delusions, had said that she wanted to kill her children. There were two previous entries in social services files that the mother had tried to strangle her first-born child. However, the decision to hold a child protection conference took a further two months and the conference did not take place until five months after that. The child's name was placed on the Child Protection Register but it then took a further five months for a social worker to be allocated. The mother subsequently drowned the child.[6]

Concern for the child's safety evidently did reach a critical threshold for the health visitor, but it is unclear whether her level of concern was communicated to social services and whether it was then put together with the previous history of the mother's attempts to strangle her older child. It is also uncertain whether lack of resources locally influenced the delays and social services' readiness to acknowledge the seriousness of the risk, especially in the light of the child being incorporated into the mother's delusions (see Chapter 3).

> Another child's father regularly abused drugs and the mother was a chronic heroin addict. The couple's relationship was unstable and characterised by violence and repeated separations. There were at least two referrals expressing concern about the parents' drug taking and its effect on the child, one made to the health visitor and the other to the NSPCC. However, this second referral was passed on to the health visitor and no statutory assessment was made. A few days later, the 2½-year-old girl was taken to hospital, having ingested methadone. Although the hospital social worker commented to the mother about the impact of her lifestyle on her ability to meet the child's needs, the principal assessment was of the child's physical state and she was discharged the next day. Over the next sixteen months, the mother repeatedly moved with her daughter to a

refuge, temporary homes and squats and then to a caravan. During that time, there was evidence that the mother spent most of her money on drugs and her life was chaotic. The child may have been sexually abused by a stranger in a toilet and was noted to be bruised, while her mother increasingly left her with different people. She died aged 3 years 7 months after ingesting her mother's methadone.[20]

We have already discussed in Chapter 3 that adults who abuse drugs can be adequate parents when they comply with treatment but that those who default from treatment programmes pose significant risks to their children. Particular problems arise as a result of their chaotic lifestyle, which may include flight from contact with helping agencies, placing the child with numerous unsuitable caretakers and other neglectful behaviour. As Swadi (1994) has discussed, the impact of the parents' general lifestyle on the child, as well as the risk posed to them during their parents' altered mental states, need to be considered. Although such concerns did arise in this case, they never progressed as far as a full assessment and therefore never reached a threshold of concern.

The first two vignettes represent unusual examples in this review because child protection conferences were called. By contrast, we found that in the majority of cases such conferences did not play a major part in the professional responses. The relative absence of child protection conferences appeared to result from professionals' thresholds of concern not being reached and so they did not consider the case to be one in which there was a risk of significant harm. In addition, they seemed to have lost sight of the intention of case conferences generally, which is to bring concerns together and consider whether the combined information reaches a threshold of concern. By pooling various professional views, previously held in isolation, a new picture has the opportunity to emerge and to indicate more clearly whether a child protection plan is needed.

We may have implied so far that there is a single threshold of concern for any case. In practice, professional responses need to evolve through a series of steps, reflecting increasing levels of concern which demand different actions. For instance, at one threshold it becomes evident that a strategy meeting should be called. A further threshold would have to be passed for a formal child protection conference to be called, which itself may result in sufficient concerns coming together for the child's name to be placed on the Child Protection Register and a child protection plan to be developed.

The number of children's names newly entered on to Child Protection Registers annually in England tends to remain fairly constant. However, there is considerable variation across different local authorities, ranging between 9 and 98 per 10,000 children (Government Statistical Service 1997). This implies major differences in criteria for critical thresholds of concern. In this study, we found only a small number of the children had their names on Child Protection Registers at the time of their death and many had not entered the child protection system. This suggests that there needs to be greater readiness amongst professionals to make the transitions from one level of concern to another.

Warnings unrecognised

It is now well documented that abusing families can give overt or covert warnings of escalating abuse which, in some instances, are indicators that the child is in imminent danger of a fatal assault. Some authors have used the term 'warning signs' to refer to general indicators of risk on a checklist (e.g. Greenland 1987; Department of Health 1991). We prefer to confine it to behaviour by parents that is a direct or disguised admission that they are severely abusing their child.

In the *Beyond Blame* study, we noted some cases in which a parent had given a disguised admission that abuse was critically escalating. The warning nature of these incidents only emerged in reviewing each case, when it was apparent that they had been followed a few days later by the child's death. In two families, parents' requests for their child to go into Care came only days before that child was fatally assaulted, while in a third case it was followed by the child running away and dying of exposure and drowning. In a fourth case, the mother asked a hospital to admit her child to investigate his 'tendency to fall' just a week before he was killed. In a fifth case, one of the children had been admitted to hospital with gastroenteritis only a few days before he was almost fatally assaulted by his father: the parents volunteered to hospital staff that he had recently fallen off the bed and also the bathstand had collapsed while the father was bathing him and he had dropped him in panic. In a sixth case, the week before a child sustained near fatal injuries, his foster mother stopped the health visitor in the street and asked her what medical conditions caused bruising, because she was being accused of beating her child. In the weeks preceding a child's death in a seventh case, the foster mother repeatedly told the child minder and general practitioner about her own severe headaches.

There has been reference to equivalent phenomena in the literature. Resnick (1969) reviewed the literature on filicide and found that 40 per cent of the parents had seen a psychiatrist or physician shortly before the crime. D'Orban (1979) interviewed 89 women charged with killing or attempting to murder their child and found that 50 has suffered minor psychiatric symptoms, such as depression, irritability, exhaustion or apathy, prior to the offence and 47 were in contact with their GP, a psychiatrist, social worker or health visitor at the time of the offence. Bennie and Sclare (1969) report that five of ten physically abusing parents had seen a doctor immediately preceding the assault, including to complain about the child's behaviour and to seek help in management. Korbin (1989) interviewed nine women imprisoned for abuse and neglect of children who had subsequently died: three had either contacted a paediatrician or another family member a few days before the child died, including expressing concerns about the child's safety. Mogielnicki *et al.* (1977) discuss three parents who attended a casualty department with chest pain, limb weakness, headache or visual blurring. Psychiatric interviews with the parents revealed that they harboured fears of being violent to their child or were actually inflicting harm on the child.

Oppenheimer (1981) presents a young mother who, ten days after taking an overdose, asked an adult psychiatrist to see her irritable 2-year-old child and her cohabitee. Six weeks later, the cohabitee fatally assaulted the child and post-mortem evidence was found of severe physical abuse that had predated the outpatient visit. In another case, a mother suffocated her child after expressing fears for many months that the child would be taken away from her.

Ounsted and Lynch (1976) refer to 'open warnings', which are more explicit evidence of maltreatment offered by some parents prior to a violent attack, including taking the child to a doctor and displaying bleeding or bruising. An example cited by Lynch and Roberts (1982) is of a mother who, two weeks prior to a severe assault, had shown her GP minor bruising that she had caused to the buttocks of her 10-week-old infant in a 'feeding battle'. Oppenheimer's paper (1981) also includes reference to a mother who attempted to strangle her infant following her discharge from a psychiatric unit, having stated on admission that she feared she would harm the child. The covert warnings that we have identified differ somewhat from these open warnings, being more masked and requiring the professional to translate the presentation into risk of child abuse.

Since completing the study into inquiry reports, we have come across a number of examples of covert warnings in our own practice that confirm the need for increased awareness of their relevance for assessing the risk to children (Reder and Duncan 1995a). One young mother called out her GP on a Saturday because her baby had 'slipped off her knee'. The doctor reassured her that the baby was physically well. The following day, the mother presented herself and her baby to the emergency psychiatric service requesting admission because she was extremely anxious. However, the mother and baby were discharged after the weekend and two days later she severely assaulted the child, fracturing his skull. In another example, a baby had been born prematurely and spent his first few weeks in the special care baby unit. Following his discharge, the mother returned repeatedly to the hospital casualty department, reporting that there was something wrong with him. Physical examination was apparently normal and she was considered to be overanxious and was reassured that the baby was well. The fourth time that she came to casualty was with a dead baby, who was later found to have seven broken sewing needles embedded in his fontanelle, neck and spine.

We were therefore interested to pursue these observations during this present study and found further manifestations of covert warnings given in the days or weeks preceding the fatal assault.

The day before a father with alcoholic hallucinosis killed two of his children, he took the eldest daughter to the GP with stomach pains, went around to the offices of a child psychologist to apologise for being drunk and aggressive in her office six months previously and asked to have an appointment with a psychiatrist. On the day of the fatal assaults, he visited his GP's surgery and asked for an appointment later in the day.[17]

The day before a mother strangled her 2-week-old baby, she telephoned the midwife to demand her approval to give up breastfeeding immediately that night. The known history was that this mother had been physically and sexually abused and looked after by the local authority during childhood and her first child had failed to thrive.[29]

In both these cases, it was the unusualness of the behaviour and its sense of urgency, together with the history of parental care and control conflicts, that might have offered a clue that the incidents heralded a crisis.

In two further cases, the parents' anxiety seemed disproportionate to the problem that they presented.

Although the baby's death was not recorded as a child abuse fatality, the post-mortem was highly suspicious and, the day before he died, his mother spoke on the telephone to the health visitor and said she wanted to ask her about a scratch on the baby's toe and a mark on his head.[43]

A few weeks before a mother threw her baby out of the window whilst suffering from post-natal depression, she told her community psychiatric nurse about her fears that the child would be removed if she was deemed not to be coping and some days later she anxiously asked the health visitor to watch her bathe the baby.[24]

We found two examples of a parent spontaneously volunteering indications of child maltreatment, only to deny it or to displace responsibility elsewhere.

Three months before a mother's cohabitee fatally assaulted her 10-month-old son, she volunteered to a neighbour that her GP had questioned her about bruising to the child and she implied that the child had been hit. Then, three weeks before he died, the child was admitted to hospital with a 'rash' that was later considered to indicate attempted strangulation, and the mother told her own father how upset she had been that the nurse said it could have been caused by a severe smack.[7]

In the middle of an assessment of her parenting capacity, a mother telephoned the assessment unit to say she had been throwing the child in the air but failed to catch her. She later told the unit's staff that she had been twirling her daughter around and the child had put her foot down and twisted it. She was considered to be co-operative and open because she had not concealed the injuries. Then, six weeks before she smothered the child, she told her social worker that her sister was pregnant and suggested that the sister would not be able to cope. Six days before the death, she told the social worker that her sister was continually shouting at and hitting her children.[31]

There were numerous examples of direct and overt warnings by parents that they were abusing their children. Most often, these were statements to social workers or health visitors that the children cried constantly and that they were smacking them, or that they could not cope generally. Some mothers used phrases such as 'at the end of my tether'. More overt evidence of wishing to be separate from the child included admitting that the child was being left in the care of others, or repeatedly asking for the child to be accommodated or adopted.[1, 2]

In one case, there appeared to be both overt and covert warnings.

The mother suffered from a paranoid psychosis, with delusions that the social worker had come to take her daughter away, and threatened to kill anyone who removed the daughter. Over the four years of the child's life, the mother made eleven requests for rehousing, fourteen attendances at her GP complaining that the child had a minor ailment and a further thirty-two GP visits with her own minor ailments. She made repeated requests for day care, a nursery place, accommodation or full care by the local authority because she was finding the child a handful and volunteered that, when she felt depressed, she wanted to harm her and she had previously tried to strangle another child of hers. Six months before she killed the child, she made another threat to kill both the child and her own mother and then sent the police and fire brigade around to her mother's home.[6]

In the warnings discussed so far, there appears to have been a wish to make professionals aware that there was a childcare problem, although its nature and severity was disguised and the warning was sometimes very subtle. There were other cases in which we were suspicious that parents had presented their child to professionals with symptoms of illness while masking the fact that they were themselves causing it.

One mother expressed excessive concern that her 2-month-old child was not responsive to light or sound and maintained this anxiety despite repeated reassurance. This was followed three months later by an account of a choking fit and an apnoeic attack and, nine months after that, by the child's admission to hospital with cigarette burns, said to have been caused 'during a robbery'.[28]

In another case, an elder child was seen by the GP thirty-two times in two years, and the mother's second child was taken to hospital unconscious from hypoglycaemia following diarrhoea and vomiting, yet no metabolic cause was found.[13]

Three months before a mother smothered her 19-month-old daughter and 5-month-old son, she took the son to the accident and emergency department saying that he had stopped breathing and gone limp.[5]

In a different case, the child's name had been entered on the Child Protection Register for neglect but his death was officially recorded as due to SIDS. At two months of age, which was two months before he died, he had been taken by his parents to the GP with screaming and 'breath holding' episodes.[42]

The term Munchausen syndrome-by-proxy has been used for parents who induce illness in their children in an attempt to satisfy their own needs through contact with medical staff (Meadow 1982; Gray and Bentovim 1996; Loader and Kelly 1996) and an association is now well recognised between abuse in the family and children presenting with symptoms such as apnoeic attacks, cyanosis or fits which defy diagnosis (Meadow 1990; Southall *et al.* 1997).

The realisation that parents may give covert warnings about abuse means that professionals must remain sensitive to this possibility, perhaps even maintaining a degree of suspiciousness. We are of the opinion that, alongside working in partnership with parents, professionals must retain an attitude of 'curiosity' towards them in order to remain sensitive to the possibility of child maltreatment. For instance, they might ask themselves: 'Why am I being told this now?' and 'Is the parent making a disguised reference to themselves?'. This does not necessarily mean reducing their supportive or partnership activities, since the stances can be complementary.

Awareness that families may also give overt warnings of child abuse means that practitioners must be prepared to take seriously statements about not being able to cope or requests for a child to live elsewhere. In particular, these admissions need to be seen as an indication of the need for further assessment.

Assessment paralysis

For completeness, assessment paralysis is mentioned again here as the other example of assessment problems which we noted running through the cases (see Chapter 3). In a number of instances, when professionals visited the home to assess a parent who was displaying evidence of irrational thought process and unpredictable behaviour, concerns about the child's safety became obscured by their primary focus on the parent's psychiatric diagnosis. It was as though their capacity to think about the safety of the child had become paralysed as a result of preoccupations about the parent.

Improving assessments

The number and variety of assessment problems running through the cases is both striking and concerning. Furthermore, problems in the assessment process were also a major theme in the *Beyond Blame* study and this suggests that there is a need to address assessment in child protection work generally. In order to consider how assessments could be improved, we shall first reflect on the principles that underlie it and then discuss how these principles might be applied in practice. However, it does need to be emphasised that we are here elaborating beyond the direct inferences of the review of 'Part 8' cases and are making more wide-ranging observations about child protection practice.

Principles of assessment

When abuse is suspected, statutory agencies must ensure that appropriate steps are taken to protect any child who might be at risk. Practitioners must actively seek out information that will help them evaluate whether parenting has broken down and decide whether to promote family separation or cohesion. An appraisal of the problems should guide the choice of response and this entails gathering relevant information and making coherent sense of it. In other words, assessment should precede intervention and the purpose of assessment is to guide action.

Practitioners must develop a mindset which incorporates this premise and which forms the foundation of all their child protection work. We would refer to it as a 'dialectic' mindset which, despite its somewhat esoteric connotations, seems to be the closest fit to the way of thinking that we are trying to convey. The term 'dialectic' was originally associated with Socrates' school of philosophy, which promoted the acquisition of knowledge through dialogue and argument. It was further developed by Hegel, who taught that a higher understanding could emerge from the comparison of contradictory arguments. This is often characterised as *thesis–antithesis–synthesis*, although thesis and hypothesis tend to be used interchangeably. These ideas are the foundation of most judicial systems, which hold that 'truth' will emerge from the balancing of opposing arguments or conflicting versions of events. It is also the basis of scientific method, which sets out to confirm or refute an original hypothesis by testing whether the counter-proposition, or 'null hypothesis', is valid.

Assessments carried out by helping professionals should not be seen as striving to arrive at a 'truth'; a 'greater understanding' is the more acceptable aim. However, the discipline imposed by dialectic thinking is a valuable context for undertaking such work. Through it, we can propose that greater understanding about any referred problem emerges in the following way. Knowledge builds up as a result of observations, which lead to the development of hypotheses, to which alternative possible hypotheses are added; the validity of these are then tested, which enables more refined hypotheses to be evolved – and so on. Reference to literature containing research findings, theoretical ideas or practical experiences informs the process at each stage. The same principles then underpin the application of knowledge to practice. Put at its simplest, assessment comes before action and the impact of actions needs to be monitored. Therefore, assessment should be an evolving process in which thought and action are reciprocal. Actions are guided by thought and the consequences of actions are noted, considered and fed back in order to influence further action (see Figure 5.1).

Such a mindset facilitates thinking about the range of likely influences on the development of a family's problems. It not only helps practitioners rank the difficulties in order of priority and suggests the various way they could respond, but also helps them to distinguish between assessment and intervention.

Another aspect of this mindset is that assessments should be based

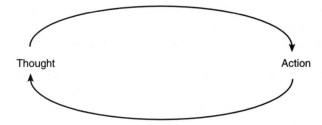

Figure 5.1 Circularity between thought and action in assessment

on a set of theoretical constructs that guide the type of information needed and the sense that can be made of it. The theoretical framework should be a central reference point for selecting the observations to be made, formulating appropriate questions and giving meaning to the responses. Otherwise, the assessment is directionless and generates a mass of discrete pieces of information that cannot be organised or understood. Absence of a framework also prevents workers from being able to rank the information in order of relevance and to distinguish between that which is relevant and that which is incidental.

In addition, assessments require criteria against which to compare findings. These could be accepted norms within a society, such as the boundary between strict limit setting and over-punitive chastisement, or threshold standards evolved through research, such as risk factors for abuse. Some standards are socially determined and some evolve through case law, but workers need to be conversant with them and their relevance. Similarly, practitioners need to keep their minds open to the possibility that the information available to them has reached a critical threshold of concern, a transitional point that demands different action.

Within a dialectic mindset, 'inquiry', 'investigation' and 'assessment' are synonymous, since they require the same basic approach, even though different circumstances may demand that different categories of information are sought and different levels of exploration are undertaken. For instance, crisis assessments of risk are very different from planned assessments of general parenting ability. Assessment of whether a child can be rehabilitated home after being cared for by others may require new areas to be addressed because the family circumstances have changed: the child will be older; there may be a new partner whose background and parenting attitudes need to be known; a parent may have engaged in a course of treatment; and so on. Nonetheless, the thinking that guides the work in any of these contexts should be the same.

In summary, we see assessment as the intermediary between hearing about a problem and deciding what should be done about it. It is a way of thinking, as well as doing, and a process of gathering, collating and appraising information and comparing the findings with accepted criteria for action. It includes formulating, testing, revising or refining hypotheses as necessary. It helps to differentiate high risk from low risk situations and it guides the choice of intervention.

From principles to practice

The implications of a dialectic mindset for a practitioner undertaking assessments are brought together in Figure 5.2. When receiving the initial referral information, practitioners should be clear who is saying what about whom and able to distinguish the referrer's opinions from their observations. This leads practitioners to develop rudimentary hypotheses of their own about the problem, to which they add information gathered from other sources and through direct observation of the family and interviews with them. They then need to consider various alternative explanations and arrive at a synthesis. The synthesis, sometimes also referred to as a formulation, is the best judgement that can be made on the basis of information available at the time. It allows assessors to consider whether a critical threshold of concern has been reached and to set their inferences against recognised thresholds for action.

One possible conclusion could be that further assessment is required, perhaps by someone else with different areas of expertise, with the inferences so far identifying the outstanding questions that remain to be explored. If practitioners are unsure what action to take, they can think through possible alternatives and the advantages and disadvantages of each. Whatever interventions are decided upon, these must be monitored, including against agreed criteria for the success or failure of that plan of action. If the conclusion of the assessment is for no further action at that time, this decision needs to be communicated with relevant others and entered in case files clearly to ensure that the thinking behind it can be understood. Of course, the decision to take no further action is itself an intervention that needs to be monitored. Figure 5.2 emphasises that the assessor's theoretical framework and practice experience, as well as teachings from previous research and the

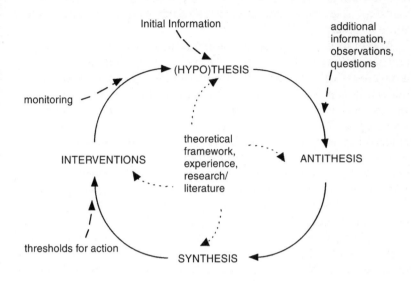

Figure 5.2 The assessment process within a 'dialectic' mindset

literature, contribute to thought and action at each phase of the process.

As discussed in Chapter 1, in our view, the most useful theoretical principles are those within an interactional framework that portray individuals as existing in relation to other people and functioning within a social and relational context. Their history helps to describe who they are and further evidence can be found in the pattern of their current relationships with significant others. In practice, this framework guides professionals to integrate historical and contemporary information about the family, its functioning, problems and relationships. The framework will also help clarify the processes that need to change for the problem to abate and hence it guides the choices of intervention and criteria used to monitor their effectiveness.

Impediments to thinking

What might interfere with the thinking components of assessment? The *Beyond Blame* study suggested a series of factors in practitioners' working contexts that had a profound impact on their handling of cases. These included gaps in training and experience, agency reorganisations, stressful working conditions, excessively heavy workloads and fixed beliefs about particular families or the nature of child abuse in general.

Absent or inadequate supervision was also highlighted as an important contributory factor. We are aware from our own everyday discussions with members of various professions that supervision is frequently approached as a mechanistic encounter in which the supervisee's case list is scrutinised for any outstanding decisions and instructions given by the supervisor for the practitioner to carry out. Undertaken in this way, its aim is merely organisational. We would suggest that the mindset that underpins assessment is equally applicable to the process of supervision, which should integrate thought and action. The supervisory process should be considered as a process of thinking between the two participants out of which relevant decisions will emerge. If practitioners understand why they are carrying out a particular activity they are more likely to own it and do it effectively. Everyday experience suggests that when someone carries out someone else's idea, they tend to do so mechanically and without the flexibility to respond to feedback.

Thinking about assessments during supervision might include organising available information into a genogram and chronology, creating an 'eco-map' of the professional network, or discussing how to apply a theoretical model to the information in order to rank it in order of importance. Such thinking would enable outstanding questions to be raised, so that the process of organising what is known leads to identification of what currently remains unknown.

Balanced thinking about complex cases can be further facilitated for front-line workers by consultation with an outside agency, such as a Child and Family Consultation Centre. This does not mean that the consultant takes over the case, or even necessarily sees the family, but offers a time for the practitioner to discuss a case in confidence. The history can be collated, an overview of the whole case obtained, priorities balanced and new ideas for action considered.

The principles of assessment that we have identified should be core components of professional training programmes, since a dialectic mindset and a relevant theoretical framework need to be acquired during training, and their practical derivatives rehearsed for many years afterwards. We shall consider this further in the final chapter, when discussing the training implications of our study.

Practice issues

We have argued in this chapter that assessment is a process of thinking as well as of action. The necessary practical skills include observational and interviewing techniques, as well as abilities to facilitate inter-professional case discussions and to present information to others. We have kept our emphasis here on the thinking component of assessment, since it underpins the application of technical skills.

However, a number of practical implications can be summarised. We believe that practice is enhanced if professionals:

- base all decisions about interventions on assessments;
- recognise the context of their assessment – e.g. whether it is to ascertain the immediate risk of harm to the child or is part of a planned procedure to consider parenting in general;
- clarify their objective – e.g. whether it is to consider the child's physical development, the child's psychological well-being, the child's safety, or the parent's mental state;
- are conversant with a theoretical framework which informs their thinking and helps integrate their observations and information;
- monitor whether they hold any fixed beliefs which could influence their assessment and prejudice their inferences – e.g. that the child will be safe as long as the father is present in the household;
- avoid prejudging the outcome of their investigation – e.g. that the child *will* return home from alternative care;
- summarise the family structure and history by drawing a genogram;
- create an 'eco-map' of the professional network involved with the family;
- integrate information about the case by compiling a chronology of the history of the family and its problems, interwoven with the history of professional involvement and the effectiveness of their attempted interventions;
- make efforts to see all relevant current caretakers;
- seek information from other relevant people – e.g. past caretakers, the extended family, members of the professional network;
- see and talk to the child, at least within 24 hours of any emergency referral;
- consider whether to hold a case discussion/conference and clarify its nature and purpose;
- consider whether there is evidence of significant harm to the child or risk of significant harm in the future;

- consider whether the risks can be contained and, if so, how;
- consider what interventions are possible and most appropriate if the risks to the child are too high;
- think through the information about a complex case with their supervisor or an outside consultant.

6   The review process

In both the original study of public inquiry reports and this present one of 'Part 8' Review reports we were interested to extend our analysis beyond the cases to include the inquiry/review process itself. We have commented in *Beyond Blame* and elsewhere (Reder and Duncan 1996) on our concerns about the old inquiry procedure and shall briefly summarise them here. Since the 'Part 8' Review process was intended to be an improvement on that system, we shall go on to reflect on its benefits and limitations as they appeared to us during this study. Then, we shall propose modifications which might enhance the process further.

The public inquiries

We have argued that, on balance, the benefits of the public inquiries were outweighed by their limitations and drawbacks. On the positive side, they undoubtedly helped raise public and professional awareness about child maltreatment and pointed to the need for formalised structures to facilitate inter-professional liaison and decisions about childcare. These included the introduction of child protection conferences, Child Protection Registers and Area Child Protection Committees and revised legislation.

However, it is doubtful whether their findings made a lasting impact upon day-to-day practice in certain crucial areas since a number of problems recurred through the years. For example, there had been an ongoing concern about communication failures between involved professionals. Although the inquiry panels had made some useful recommendations about the structures necessary for good communication and the mechanics of information recording and transfer, they did not address the psychology of communication in which the meaning attributed to the words of a message changes according to contextual and interrelationship factors.

Public inquiries were also very costly in both financial and personal terms. One reputedly cost half a million pounds. Many were used for disciplinary purposes and the impact of the adversarial proceedings, often dramatically reported in the media, reverberated through individual workers' lives, their agencies and professions for years afterwards, leading to self-reproach or defensive practice with other families.

We believe that these drawbacks to the public inquiries arose because of the conflicting expectations of them. They appeared to have been set up to serve diverse purposes, most especially: to apportion blame to involved professionals and discipline them; to learn from the cases in order to improve child protection practice; to reassure the public that the state is concerned about child welfare; and to provide an opportunity for catharsis of society's horror at child maltreatment. While each agenda could be considered to be legitimate in its own right, the inquiry process seemed unable to satisfy the different pressures and interests or to reconcile the contradictory aims.

The incompatibility between a desire to learn from the cases and an intention to discipline workers was particularly striking. We had the impression that there was a crucial lack of clarity about these conflicting agendas throughout most of the public inquiries and that the tension impacted on the panels themselves, as well as the professionals invited to give evidence. Some panels split around this issue, resulting in minority reports, while professionals increasingly declined to appear before them, fearing hostile accusations and blame. We would contend that a worker giving an account of their involvement on a case as part of a learning exercise inevitably provides very different information, and with a different emphasis, from one giving evidence in the adversarial atmosphere of a disciplinary hearing. The defensive self-interest necessary for proceedings with disciplinary overtones is incompatible with the open exploration required for understanding and learning.

More recently, we have become aware of another context which constrains freedom to learn. Increasingly, professionals and their employing agencies are exposed to allegations of negligence and the risk of litigation. They are therefore being advised to adopt a cautious and self-protective approach to case reviews. For instance, mental health trusts are tightening up their procedures for 'serious incident inquiries' following a patient's suicide or violence to a member of the public. Although a principal aim of such inquiries is to learn from the cases, legal advisers are warning of the possible consequences of uncensored disclosure to the patient's family.

The 'Part 8' Review system

In many ways, the 'Part 8' Review system has been an improvement on the earlier public inquiries. There has appeared to be a greater determination by those conducting them to learn policy and practice lessons from the tragedies and the conduct of the reviews has seemed far less adversarial and acrimonious. This, in turn, has facilitated the emergence of learnable lessons, at least in some cases. However, there were times during this study that we closed a file with a sigh, commenting to each other that we still understood little about the case and that it seemed unlikely that the review would have made a significant difference to local practice. We shall examine in some detail the factors that left us with certain misgivings about the 'Part 8' Review process in its current form.

It is important to acknowledge that we approached the Review files with the preoccupations of practising clinicians who use an interactional model to make sense of people's behaviour. We were also drawing on our own practice experiences in the area of child protection and upon the academic literature to weigh up the available information and form our own judgements. We were therefore looking to find sufficient information about each case to allow us to apply our theoretical model and to understand the family's functioning and the professional network's response to it. Clearly, a study team who used a different theoretical model or who had a different professional background, such as in law, or administration, or politics, might have focused on different aspects of the cases and come to different conclusions about the review process. Nonetheless, we believe that the concerns of practising clinicians are especially relevant in these cases, since the reviews are intended in whole or in part to feed back into everyday practice and improve professional work.

Limitations of the review process

It is evident that 'Part 8' Reviews do not give an accurate picture of the number of fatal child abuse cases across the country and are, at best, only a representative sample. Some cases are included in the procedure and notified to the Department of Health because the children had been in the care of the local authority, even though they certainly died from a chronic medical condition. Other notified cases are not identified as child maltreatment, even though there could be consider-able grounds for drawing that inference. Clearly, coroners' verdicts of 'misadventure', 'accidental death' or 'natural causes' are critical in determining whether there will be criminal prosecution and whether case reviews will be held and we were left concerned that a number of abuse deaths may be missed, particularly among those which receive a diagnosis of SIDS.

We found a few cases which would not have received a 'Part 8' Review but for a local professional's persistent demands for one. In one case, a paediatrician pressed for a review because he believed that a child's death from cystic fibrosis had been hastened by chronic neglect. In another, a paediatrician was concerned that the pathologist had minimised the relevance of a subdural haematoma found at post-mortem. One child's death was recorded as 'bronchitis', when the case history suggested that she had been rented out by drug-dependent parents to a neighbour who drugged her during sexual abuse.

Once a decision had been taken to proceed to a 'Part 8' Review, it was apparent that a great deal of time, effort and emotional investment went into conducting it, with obvious attempts by local reviewers to do justice to the complexities of the case. However, despite this, we concluded that the practical value of their reports was sometimes limited by a number of factors. These included the perceived purpose of the procedure, the composition of the panels, the processing of the information that was available and the presentation style of the final reports.

Many reviewers limited their focus to whether the existing child protection procedures had been followed during work on the case. Often, they concluded that, since the procedures had been adhered to, the tragedy could not have been foreseen and there was little that could have been done to prevent it. It is not clear whether such concern with procedures was due to misunderstandings about the intentions behind 'Part 8' Reviews, was a defensive approach to the task, or was based on a belief that complying with policies is all that is needed. In our view, it is necessary for practitioners to do more than merely follow proce-dures: what also matters is how they think about, interpret and apply them, as well as find them relevant to the circumstances under consid-eration.

The reviewers who concentrated on whether procedures were followed produced recommendations which were equally restricted in scope. There was only a small number of cases in which we felt that wide-ranging lessons for practice, such as approaches to assessment, had been identified. One report did highlight a series of assessment factors that had been missed and another pointed to the need for joint assessments between adult mental health professionals and children's services when a parent manifests signs of psychiatric disorder.

This limited focus may be partly explained by the membership and level of expertise of the review panels, which varied considerably from case to case. In only one instance did it appear that an independent outside expert had been brought in. Surprisingly, some panels did not include a representative of the only profession which could have shed light on crucial aspects of the case. For example, there was no medical member on a panel reviewing the death of a child whose skin lesions suggested attempted strangulation, nor on the one in which a paediatrician had urged a case review because of suspicious post-mortem findings. There was no psychiatrist on the panel reviewing a case in which four psychiatrists had seen the parent for assessment and treatment after she had murdered her first child.

A great deal of crucial information, at least for us as clinicians who believe that current functioning is best understood in the context of personality development and past relationships, was unfortunately not available in the reports. In the majority of cases, only passing reference was made to the parents' background history and most reviews tended not to supplement the question 'What do we know?' (from the information available) with 'What do we *not* know?' (so that the case can be better understood). Our strong impression was that information that had not been sought during work with the case remained unknown by the review panels and there appeared to have been no active steps to acquire missing details that might have helped them better understand the case. One example of this was a family in which the father had been present in the household throughout the child's life but was hardly mentioned in the report, as though he had not played a part in childcare. If that had indeed been the mindset of the original workers, we would have expected the review panel to have challenged it. Another review reported 'case conference held' but gave no details about its nature, membership, discussion or conclusions, although they were presumably available in the agency files.

One notable factor contributing to the absence of relevant information was that a number of agencies involved in the cases did not participate in the reviews. There was no psychiatric service contribution to two reviews where the caretakers had manifest significant mental health problems. General practitioners declined to contribute to two reviews, while, in a third, their management system refused to participate. Trade union influence meant that social services did not submit a report in one case because the staff had been criticised in a previous review. Social services only submitted monthly summaries of their work to one review and, in another, had incorporated all the other agency activities into their chronology, as though it were theirs. The paediatrician who had pressed for one case to be reviewed did not then contribute to the actual process. Concurrent criminal proceedings also limited police participation in a number of instances.

We encountered difficulty collating the information that was contained in a number of files. Sometimes this was because facts given in different places did not correspond or the different agencies had submitted different levels of detail. Integrated chronologies giving an overview of the whole case were absent from three files, which instead held separate agency reports only. One file consisted only of the ACPC's conclusions, without details of the case, while two others consisted only of a single agency's chronology and review.

There was no standardised format for the presentation of the reports and some reviewers put considerable effort into drawing up a table so that each agency's activities over the course of the case could be read side by side. Unfortunately, this was extremely difficult to read, since the tables contained numerous repetitions in different sections, and ultimately this style proved unhelpful. It was unusual to find an attempt at a genogram and, when one was included, it did not comply with recognised nomenclature. A number of reviewers assumed that the readership would have local knowledge, so that agencies were referred to in the report by name only, without clarifying their function and status. Others referred to people by their initials, which made for confusing reading, or by their name without reference to their profession or role.

In summary, we felt that our ability to understand the dynamics of the cases or draw wide-ranging practice lessons from them was restricted by flexibilities in the current review procedure and the varying ways it is being applied. Over the years, the main preoccupation appears to have shifted from blaming individuals for failing to prevent a child's death to minimising responsibility because all procedures were followed. Neither position is likely to further significantly our understanding of severe child abuse and a more neutral middle course is likely to be more fruitful.

Requirements of a review procedure

The difficulties we encountered in reviewing this series of cases help us to identify the likely requirements of an improved system (Reder and Duncan 1998). The system should allow all child deaths to be considered so that abuse-related fatalities are not missed. Reviews would be best conducted by an independent expert or small team of experts, who have considerable practice experience and can articulate a framework within which they will attempt to make sense of the events. Such a team would require sufficient time to do justice to the information and complexities of the circumstances. They should be furnished with details of the involvement of all relevant agencies, who would be obliged to contribute to any review. A more standardised format for the review and report would be helpful, including a comprehensive genogram and integrated chronology of all agencies' knowledge of, and work with, the family. The chronology should be in text form, giving dates of events and detailed summaries of what happened. The review team would be able to seek out missing information and resolve inconsistencies. In addition, the procedure should enable all the potentially conflicting agendas consequent on a child abuse death to be satisfied and should also recognise that different levels of learning may be necessary.

The principles behind any system should correspond to the dialectic mindset that we have discussed in the previous chapter, and, in a sense, undertaking a case review could mirror the process of thinking that underpins assessments. It can be traced through with reference to Figure 5.2, where the initial information is news that a child has died. This should activate a procedure that attempts to understand why this happened and seeks information from those involved in order to consider various possible explanations. A synthesis understanding is then compiled into a report, which also addresses whether thresholds for action – such as risk factors or child protection guidelines – were acknowledged and their implications followed. The reviewers' intervention by way of their recommendations would then be monitored and, if necessary, refined in the light of future experience.

Before proposing a revised model that incorporates these requirements, we shall consider procedures which have been established for equivalent reviews in the United States of America and the United Kingdom. These include the Child Death Review Teams in the USA, and, in the UK, the Leeds Inquiries into Infant Deaths and the Confidential Inquiry into Homicides and Suicides by Mentally Ill People.

Child Death Review Teams were pioneered by Michael Durfee in Los Angeles during the late 1970s and currently forty-five states have local and/or state-wide teams (Durfee 1989; Durfee *et al.* 1992; US Advisory Board on Child Abuse and Neglect 1995; Gellert *et al.* 1995; Durfee and Tilton-Durfee 1995). The membership, terms of reference and practice vary in different localities, but their common purpose is to understand and prevent fatal child abuse. They review all children's deaths in which there may be any suspicion that maltreatment played a part. Increasingly, teams are being formalised under statute which facilitates their capacity to meet regularly, receive the necessary information and liaise across agencies.

In thirty-one states, the team structure has evolved so that a number of standing local teams meet to review individual cases, while a state-wide team collates their data and provides an overview across the state. The local teams usually include child welfare, criminal justice, coroner's office and medical representatives, with state teams including acknowledged professional experts, government officials and agency representatives.

In Missouri, for example, each county is required by law to have a team which conducts case-by-case reviews within 48 hours of the death of any child younger than 15 years (US Advisory Board on Child Abuse and Neglect 1995). The coroner or medical examiner team member considers all the cases and passes through to a full team review any which give rise to suspicion. The state-wide team monitors and advises on policy.

California has a state team and forty-five local teams. Its Orange County team is chaired by the Deputy Coroner, who has legal authority to obtain pertinent medical records and the child protection professional members obtain files from their services (Gellert *et al.* 1995). In Los Angeles, each morning the County Coroner sends details of all child deaths during the previous 24 hours to the District Attorney's office and from there to the review team. The team cross-references with agency records, to ascertain whether there had been previous contacts, and decides which fatalities to review. Their guide is that: the child was under 10 years of age; there was evidence of abuse, including sexual; a baby was stillborn at home; a 'SIDS' death had equivocal post-mortem findings; and all cases of bathtub drowning, head trauma, burns and suicide (Durfee 1989). The Los Angeles team meets monthly and comprises approximately fifteen professionals, who consider some two hundred and fifty deaths a year but review only thirty to forty (Stewart 1995).

Many Child Death Review Teams extend their remit beyond case review and take the initiative for directing the criminal investigation and for subsequent case management, such as ensuring that the needs of surviving siblings are addressed. However, confidentiality remains within the team for all material submitted to it, so that evidence or information to be used for subsequent case action must be obtained by separate investigation or subpoena. If the team's peer review uncovers poor case management, the agency concerned is responsible for disciplinary and educational implications and conflicts of interest are said not to arise (Durfee, personal communication).

The value of the teams has been wide-ranging, including modifying procedures for data collection, highlighting demographic patterns in abuse deaths, recognising misdiagnosed deaths, confirming the significant under-reporting of fatal child abuse, detecting serial murders, raising coroners' sensitivity to abuse, enhancing criminal investigations, ensuring that appropriate support is made available to families, identifying preventive measures and promoting legislation aimed at the prevention of accidents.

Similar teams have been established in Canada and Australia (Durfee and Tilton-Durfee 1995), but the closest parallel in the UK is probably the system in Leeds described by Hobbs *et al.* (1995) where health and social services personnel conducted a detailed inquiry into each unexpected death of a child between the age of seven days and two years. Information was gathered for the inquiry by specially trained health visitors, who interviewed the family, and from hospital and GP records, and the team's aim was to assist future prevention by a better understanding of the circumstances and factors which contributed to the death. These inquiries confirmed that the deaths most often had multiple contributory factors, including biological, social and psychological, but social deprivation remained the most important associated factor.

Another precedent of considerable interest is the Confidential Inquiry into Homicides and Suicides by Mentally Ill People (Steering Committee 1996), which itself has been modelled on existing confidential inquiries into peri-operative deaths, maternal deaths and stillbirths. The homicides and suicides audit project was set up in 1992 jointly by the Department of Health and the Royal College of Psychiatrists, with the aims of collating information about the circumstances and antecedents of the deaths and generating ideas about future prevention. Relevant cases are identified by the Home Office, coroners' offices, local pathologists, Directors of Public Health and consultant psychiatrists, who notify the inquiry team. Questionnaires are sent out to the principal mental health team members concerned with that patient's care and their replies are anonymised and treated with strict confidence. This has enabled the inquiry team to identify common themes in the cases, including problems with communication, lack of clarity about care plans and needs for additional training in risk assessment – the very same issues we have identified in our two reviews of fatal child abuse cases.

Proposal for reviewing cases

The experiences of the Child Death Review Teams in the United States and inquiries into infant deaths in Leeds indicate the very real value of systems which aim to review *all* child deaths. In this way, not only are clear cases of child abuse studied, but also suspicious deaths and those which would otherwise have been missed. However, the Child Death Review Teams and the Leeds inquiries appear to focus more on the families themselves, with less attention to the functioning of professionals in the child protection network. The Homicides and Suicides Confidential Inquiry, by contrast, is particularly interested in the clinical services provided.

In proposing a national model for child abuse reviews in the UK, consideration must be given to the range of purposes for which case reviews are usually undertaken. As we have argued, each of these agendas is important but they cannot be satisfied together through a single review procedure. Instead, a process is needed that separates out the requirements and addresses each one in turn. In addition, the system must respect individuals' and employing agencies' vulnerability to the possibility of negligence claims.

If case reviews are to be used for the purpose of learning or as a disciplinary measure, they must be able to address the various levels of influence on professionals' work. These include their training, their experience, their profession's standards of practice, their supervision, their emotional support, their agency's beliefs and policies, their agency's relationships with others, their working environment, the legal context and central policies. A child's death may have occurred in the context of problems or inconsistencies at any of these levels (Reder *et al.* 1993a) and it must be possible to include all of them in the case review.

We would suggest that the wide-ranging remit of the Child Death Review Teams in the United States may not fully translate to the United Kingdom, especially with regard to their law-enforcement roles and active contributions to case management. However, there appear to be considerable advantages to a system which establishes under statute standing teams of experts to consider all child deaths and to review selected cases in greater depth. Such teams would have research and educative functions and a capacity to sharpen professional awareness and recognition of maltreatment. They could contribute to knowledge of risk factors and inter-agency functioning and inform development of central policy.

However, we found ourselves in some dilemma about the most useful and appropriate scheme within which such teams might operate in this country. Our debates centred around whether the drive by some to discipline workers or to gain redress through negligence claims would always overshadow attempts at learning. On the one hand, we are convinced that the whole professional system, from involved workers and their agencies, to other practitioners and central government, has a strong desire to maximise the educative potential of tragedies so as to reduce the possibility of recurrence (e.g. Department of Health and Social Security 1982; Department of Health 1991; Creighton 1992; Eastman 1996). But on the other hand, professional agencies are compelled to address self-protection as a priority. A system which facilitates learning would require open disclosure of information without fear of censure, while a system which satisfies self-protection needs could not expect such licence.

The dilemma revolved around issues of openness and confidentiality. We noted that information available to the Child Death Review Teams, the Leeds inquiries and the Confidential Inquiry into Homicides and Suicides was strictly confidential and not available to any outside party for whatever purpose. While the USA's review teams do concern themselves with individual cases, the two UK systems have found greater educative potential in collating patterns across cases where anonymity can also be guaranteed. We feel it is possible to resolve the dilemma about confidentiality by recognising that there are different levels of learning. Some local practice and procedural lessons can be identified from individual case reviews, despite the probability that selected information would be made available with one eye on self-protection. A parallel review process, in which the information remained strictly confidential, would be required to enable general practical and epidemiological lessons to be collated across a series of cases.

We therefore propose a system for local case reviews which allows for disciplinary considerations and a more central system running alongside it in which standing teams collate anonymous data across numbers of cases. This proposal is depicted in Figure 6.1, in which 'local' might be borough-sized localities and 'regional' the equivalent of Health Regions. We suggest the establishment, under statute, of Regional Child Death Review Teams, whose members would bring to them considerable interest and expertise in problems of child abuse. The aims of these teams would be to maintain an overview of all child

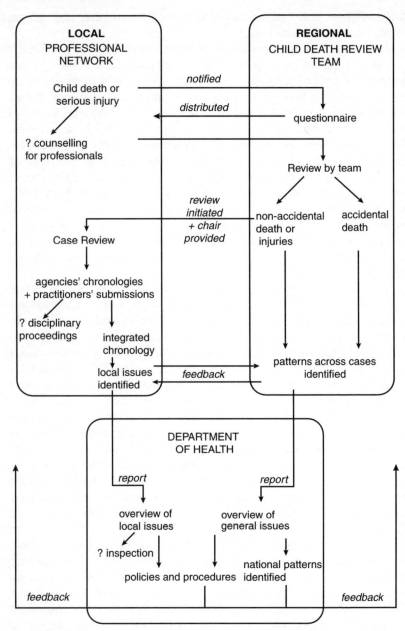

Figure 6.1 Proposed system for reviewing children's deaths

deaths in the region, to initiate local case reviews when necessary, to provide expertise to localities, such as providing the chair for a case review, and to accumulate and disseminate knowledge about child abuse.

The teams would be notified immediately about each death of, or serious injury to, a child between birth and ten years of age, the years during which the vast majority of fatal abuse occurs. A questionnaire would be circulated to the key members of the professional network involved in the case and their responses collated and reviewed by the Regional Team. This would indicate which cases contained clear or suspicious indicators that the child died from maltreatment, or that maltreatment contributed in some way to the fatality. If so, the team would initiate a local review of the case and would provide an independent chair for it.

In the meantime, in recognition of the distress that overtakes members of a professional network when a child known to them is severely injured or killed, they would be offered confidential counselling.

Cases 'referred' for local review would enter a system very much as now, in which named professionals and designated professionals in the National Health Service (Department of Health and Welsh Office 1995) and uninvolved seniors in other agencies collate the agency records and prepare a chronology of its staff's work on the case. In order to capture concerns about the functioning of managers in the agency, or about child protection policies in general, involved practitioners would also be invited to submit their own comments and observations. This material would form the basis upon which the agency or relevant profession decided that disciplinary measures should be pursued. The Chair of the Review Team would integrate all agency chronologies into a single coherent chronology and a report identifying any concerns about local practice. Information available for agency chronologies would not be confidential and might potentially be used in disciplinary or compensation proceedings.

However, the material submitted to the Regional Teams and the contents of the team's deliberations would be confidential, since their role would be to integrate patterns across cases. For this purpose, the names of the families, the professionals and the locality can be removed.

The Department of Health would receive reports of local case reviews, much as now, and would need to consider whether concerns about a particular locality's functioning required further consideration, such as through a Social Services Inspectorate visit. The

Department would also receive overview reports from the Regional Teams in order to monitor their findings and draw policy and practice inferences. In addition, the Department could collate national patterns. Feedback could occur from time to time from the Department but also from the local case reviews and studies of the Regional Teams.

It might be argued that this proposal adds another layer to the existing system, thereby complicating it and rendering it more expensive. We have felt it preferable to advise adding this regional team layer so that matters of confidentiality do not obstruct the learning process. It recognises that learning may need to take place at different levels, focusing on different issues. It also brings together professionals with expertise and interest in furthering knowledge about child maltreatment who are, in turn, able to inform the Department of Health's considerations about policies and procedures. Many elements of this system are already in place, although it would require further preparatory work to devise meaningful and useful questionnaires.

When news breaks that a child has been killed by its caretaker(s), the emotional distress is profound for all directly concerned – surviving family members, involved professionals and other agency staff – and reverberates out to the public at large. Perhaps the magnitude of this impact cannot be encapsulated in words. We would hope that a review system such as the one we have proposed could help contain some of the emotions and eventually allow the tragedy to be turned to the benefit of other children in the future.

Since finalising these study inferences, the Department of Health has consulted widely on possible revisions to the *Working Together* guidelines (Department of Health 1998) and some of their proposals arose out of our original internal report to the Department (Duncan and Reder 1997a). At the time of writing this chapter, the final format for reviewing child deaths has not yet been announced.

Practice issues

- Reviews of children's deaths would be enhanced by the inclusion on review panels of personnel from relevant professions who are of sufficient seniority and experience.
- Standing Child Death Review Teams could improve the identification of maltreatment related deaths and the practice lessons that might be learned from them.
- Participants in case reviews at all levels of seniority should be made aware of the remit of the review – i.e. whether its primary

task is disciplinary, learning, and so on.

- Case review reports should have a standard format and contain detailed genograms and family histories, together with integrated chronologies of significant events, professional interventions and their outcomes.
- Reviewers' recommendations should be clearly based on their understanding of the dynamics of the case and of the different levels of influence on professionals' work, as well as on procedural factors.

7　Prevention

Probably the most important question to arise from a study such as this is whether the ultimate tragedy of a child death can be prevented by front-line professionals. Most inquiries into tragedies are set up with the declared intention that 'this should never happen again' and this understandable wish tends to be accompanied by a presumption that they could have been avoided. For example, the inquiry into the death of Jasmine Beckford (Inquiry Report 1985) asserted that her death had been 'a predictable and preventable homicide' and went on to conclude that the blame should be shared between certain involved professionals. How realistic is this?

In this chapter, we shall discuss the difficulties that exist in forecasting child abuse fatalities because they are such rare and complex events. We shall first take an epidemiological perspective, expanding on areas of discussion presented earlier in this book, to place fatal abuse in the context of child maltreatment generally. Then we shall take a more practice-oriented approach, drawing together the attempts that have been made to identify characteristics unique to families in which fatal abuse has occurred. Finally, we shall reprise the factors that we have identified in our two studies that may offer additional pointers towards prediction.

Epidemiological perspectives

Epidemiological approaches to predicting fatal child abuse face at least four major problems. The first difficulty is that the origins of child maltreatment are multi-determined. We have already emphasised that incidents of child abuse of any severity are not merely caused by dysfunctional parents but are interactional events, occurring at moments of heightened stress in the lives of adults who suffer from unresolved conflicts and who are caring for vulnerable children.

Therefore, any attempt to predict fatal abuse should not focus exclusively on attributes of individuals but must consider complex interactional scenarios and the interplay between parent, child and circumstance.

Furthermore, it is likely that circumstances differ between various forms of fatal maltreatment. These include: abandonment of a baby at birth following a denied pregnancy; killing a baby during post-natal psychosis; the sudden shaking of an infant by its caretaker in a fit of overwhelming frustration; a murderous assault on a child by a deluded parent; induced fatal illness; smothering disguised as SIDS; and relentless neglect of an older child. In order to be practically valid, predictive procedures should be able to distinguish between the various scenarios.

Gelles (1991) has also warned that mild physical punishment, severe abuse and child homicide may be distinct behaviours rather than continuities on the same spectrum of phenomena. Indeed, there are no clear parameters for deciding what does constitute 'child abuse', which remains essentially a social construction, open to different interpretations (Reder *et al.* 1993a). When considering research studies, many epidemiological reports use the term 'child homicide' generically and do not distinguish between, for example, deaths caused within the home or by strangers.

The second problem concerns the rarity of the event. Although the occurrence of fatal child abuse in the general population is not accurately known and a significant under-reporting is widely acknowledged (Ewigman *et al.* 1993; McClain *et al.* 1993), it is undoubtedly very uncommon. Creighton and Gallagher (1988) have estimated that some 198 child deaths per annum in the United Kingdom are directly caused by, or contributed to by, abuse or neglect, while Wilczynski (1997) suggested a higher figure of 308 for England and Wales. An approximate rate for the UK can be inferred from these two estimates; perhaps 200 to 300 children die annually from abuse, out of a population of 11 million children (Department of Health 1995) – i.e. 2 to 3 per 100,000 children.

Estimates for the United States vary between 2,000 and 5,000 deaths per year (US Advisory Board on Child Abuse and Neglect 1995). McClain *et al.* (1993) proposed that as many as 11.6 per 100,000 children under four years of age die in the United States from abuse or neglect, although Levine (1996) considered that 4 per 100,000 is more realistic.

Physical abuse is the commonest cause of death, but a substantial number of neglect fatalities also occur, perhaps as many as 40 per cent of abuse related deaths (Alfaro 1988; Margolin 1990; Levine *et al.* 1994).

These figures must be set against the number of children known to child protection agencies. A series of studies, which were summarised by the Department of Health (1995), traced children through the child protection system and gave the following approximations. Of 11 million children in England, some 160,000 (1.5 per cent) are referred each year to social services for investigation of maltreatment allegations. Forty-four per cent of these referrals are for suspected physical abuse and 25 per cent for possible neglect, meaning, therefore, that approximately 1 per cent of all children are referred annually with these particular concerns. Of the 160,000 children who are referred, around 24,500 (15.3 per cent) have names newly entered on to a Child Protection Register, implying that a child protection plan is considered necessary. If 200–300 children die annually as the result of abuse, this is approximately 0.002 per cent of all children, 0.15 per cent of all referred children and around 1 per cent of all newly registered children.

The third complexity is that the majority of maltreatment deaths occur in families not previously known to child protection agencies. Although Sabotta and Davis (1992) quoted evidence that 45–55 per cent of fatally abused children had previously been reported to child protection services, other reported figures tend to be lower. According to Alfaro (1988) and Levine *et al.* (1994), only about one-third of cases in the United States had previous contact and Anderson *et al.* (1983) and Showers *et al.* (1985) suggested that it is only one-quarter. Out of fourteen fatal abuse cases known to one children's hospital (Hicks and Gaughan 1995), six families (43 per cent) had had prior protective service involvement, but the previous concerns had been about a sibling in four of them. Margolin's report (1990) that only 39 per cent of neglect fatalities in Iowa had any previous involvement with child protection services is salutary, since neglect is likely to be a more prolonged form of abuse than physical maltreatment and could be expected to come to the awareness of a range of professionals.

In the United Kingdom, Scott (1973) found that 28 per cent of fathers or father substitutes convicted of killing a child in their care were already being monitored by social agencies on account of child abuse concerns, while Creighton (1989) reported that the names of 25 per cent of children whose deaths were notified to the NSPCC between 1983 and 1987 were previously known to protective services. In Wilczynski's review (1997) of 48 cases referred to the Director of Public Prosecutions, there had been previous contact with professionals about physical abuse in only 21 per cent of cases, but eleven of seventeen surviving siblings had suffered neglect, physical or emotional abuse or suspicious prior injuries.

In our present study, the family had previously been referred to a statutory agency because of concerns about parenting in 55 per cent of the cases (46 per cent of the 'confirmed' deaths and 79 per cent of the 'suspicious' deaths). These concerns were usually directly about child protection, although some had been about a sibling. The names of nine of the children were on the Child Protection Register at the time they were killed (three of the 'confirmed' deaths and six of the 'suspicious' deaths), while the names of siblings were registered in another of the 'confirmed' cases.

Fourth, it is necessary to recognise the distinction between prediction/prevention at the primary, secondary and tertiary levels (Browne *et al* 2000). Primary prevention aims to prevent a problem before it starts and, for fatal child abuse, this would require professionals to identify potentially 'infanticidal parents' in the general population. Secondary prevention focuses on certain selected families identified as more at risk. Measures at the tertiary level attempt to minimise the consequences of the problem in those families already known to be demonstrating it: in other words, predicting which parents already known to child protection services because of child maltreatment are the ones who will fatally abuse.

In practice, most attention has been focused at the tertiary level because of social and professional concern about children dying who were already known to child protection agencies. We have therefore condensed our discussion of primary and secondary prediction in order to concentrate on the tertiary level issues.

Prediction at the primary and secondary levels

Case studies have revealed that, although only a minority of the families in which a child had died from abuse were previously known to statutory agencies, many more had had recent contact with other professionals at the time of the fatality. We have already discussed in Chapter 5 reports by Resnick (1969), d'Orban (1979) and Korbin (1989), who found that around one-half of parents who had killed their child had been in contact with a range of helping professionals immediately prior to the offence. In Wilczynski's study (1997), 44 per cent of the suspected perpetrators of a child's death had seen a medical practitioner (GP, psychiatrist or paediatrician) prior to the offence and 40 per cent had seen a social worker, although the time interval was not specified. Interestingly, the commonest reason for professional contact had been about a parent's mental health. This suggests that opportunities may arise for professionals not customarily accorded child protection responsibilities to consider childcare issues prior to a fatality.

There have been occasional reports about mothers who presented to psychiatrists with overt obsessional fears of harming their child (Anthony and Kreitman 1970; Button and Reivich 1972). The mothers were successfully treated with psychotherapy and none acted upon their murderous thoughts. However, the authors make no reference to child protective measures during the treatment, which we would consider to be essential.

One finding common to all studies, including our own, concerns the very young age of children killed. The majority of abuse fatalities are of children in the first year of life, although the heightened risk does continue into the second year (e.g. Schloesser *et al.* 1992; Hegar *et al.* 1994; Durfee and Tilton-Durfee 1995; US Advisory Board on Child Abuse and Neglect 1995). This implies that many of the mothers and children will recently have been seen by obstetric, post-natal or infant health services and that opportunities exist for preventive work around the perinatal period. We shall return to this issue later in the discussion.

Although the majority of babies are known to health professionals, a small sub-group of fatality cases concerns mothers who do not acknowledge that they are pregnant and fail to present for any ante-natal care. The baby is born in secret and is abandoned to die or is actively killed (Brozovsky and Falit 1971; Finnegan *et al.* 1982; Saunders 1989; Green and Manohar 1990; Fitzpatrick 1995), although a few babies do survive (Wilkins 1985; Cherland and Matthews 1989). Marks and Kumar (1993) found Home Office records for England and Wales of 45 neonaticides (children killed within 24 hours of birth) between 1982 and 1988 – an average of some 7 per year, being 21 per cent of all known infant homicides. The Scottish Office recorded 6 confirmed neonaticides, out of a total of 45 infanticides, between 1978 and 1993 (Marks and Kumar 1996). In Queensland, Australia, Wilkey *et al.* (1982) found 11 such cases over a ten-year period from a population of two million, out of a total of 49 child killings from all causes.

Accounts of such cases usually report therapeutic work with the mothers some time after the baby's death. The nature of the problem – in which the mother denies the pregnancy and ignores antenatal care and relatives remain unaware of the mother's state – means that professionals rarely have the opportunity to intervene before the infant is killed. However, Bonnet (1993) had the opportunity to interview a number of such mothers when they eventually acknowledged the pregnancy or soon after delivery, and uncovered denied violent fantasies towards the infants: she recommended that planned adoption at birth could prevent some neonaticides.

Prediction at the tertiary level

Here, we are concerned with the possibility of predicting which children already known to statutory agencies because of abuse will be killed by their caretakers. In addition to the estimates for the UK we have discussed earlier, a few retrospective studies have indicated the number of abused children who are killed. Wilkey *et al.* (1982) gave a figure from Brisbane of 1–2 per cent and Showers *et al.* (1985) reported that four deaths occurred in a group of 776 cases (0.5 per cent) reported to the Children's Hospital in Columbus, Ohio. The American Association for Protecting Children (1986) estimated fewer than 1 per cent but added that 11 per cent suffer life-threatening, disabling or disfiguring injuries.

Hollander (1986) and Sabotta and Davis (1992) concluded that child homicide is preceded by physical abuse at rates greater than that found generally. According to Hollander, if a child has been returned home following physical abuse: 'there should be no hesitation or delay in recommending a second removal of the child if physical abuse is noted, because physical abuse precedes a large percentage of child homicides' (Hollander 1986: 90).

Although this might be a sound principle, in practice reabuse rates are generally reported to be high, despite professional interventions. Herrenkohl *et al.* (1979) found that, among families in which physical abuse had occurred, 54 per cent showed repeat incidents in up to ten years of follow-up (the figure was 44 per cent for gross neglect). Alexander *et al.* (1990) gave a recidivism rate for all child abuse in Iowa as one-third, with a similar figure emerging from Browne's follow-up study in North Carolina (1986). Murphy *et al.* (1992) followed up maltreated children who had been restored to parental custody by the Boston Juvenile Court for two years and found that almost one-third of them had a subsequent official report of mistreatment. In half of these cases, the reabuse was so serious that the case had to return to court. Wood (1997) found lower repeat rates in El Paso in a two-year follow-up of validated child abuse/neglect cases: new allegations of physical abuse had occurred in 16 per cent of cases

(9 per cent were substantiated) and of neglect in 13 per cent (5 per cent were substantiated).

In the UK, Corby (1987) studied families receiving casework following physical abuse and neglect and found a recurrence rate of 28 per cent. Farmer and Owen (1995) discovered that 25 per cent of children whose names had been entered on the Child Protection Register for all kinds of abuse had been reabused within twenty months, while Thorburn *et al.* (1995) reported an actual or suspected reabuse rate within six months of one in five children and Gibbons *et al.* (1995) found a reabuse rate following physical abuse of 20 per cent over ten years.

From an epidemiological perspective, then, there is insufficient guidance in the literature to help us predict fatal abuse from amongst families where children are known to have been maltreated. Fatal abuse is rare, comparatively few of the families in which it does occur are known to protective agencies and reabuse rates are relatively (indeed unacceptably) high where abuse has already been identified. We therefore turn to trying to identify predictive factors from specific cases.

Case study perspectives

The two themes that we shall consider here are the value of high risk checklists and the identification of serial filicide.

High-risk checklists

Greenland (1987) reviewed child abuse fatalities from different countries and constructed a high-risk checklist from observed similarities between the cases. Factors relevant to the parents were said to be:

- previously abused/neglected as a child;
- history of abusive/neglectful parenting;
- history of criminally assaultive and/or suicidal behaviour;
- single, separated or living with a partner who is not the child's biological parent;
- poor, unemployed or received inadequate education;
- abuses alcohol and/or drugs;
- pregnant or in the post-partum period or has a chronic illness.

Factors concerning the child were:

- previously abused/neglected;
- premature, low birth weight, birth defect, chronic illness or developmental lag;
- prolonged separation from the mother;
- adopted, fostered or a stepchild;
- currently underweight; cries frequently or difficult to comfort;
- difficulties in feeding or elimination.

According to Greenland, an infant who has suffered a serious non-accidental injury remains at 'high risk' if more than half of the factors are positive. Greenland admitted that his checklist needed to be tested in everyday practice but, on closer examination, there appears to be little in the list which is specific to fatal abuse and distinguishes it from non-fatal physical maltreatment in order to act as a tertiary level guide to front-line professionals. For example, Browne has worked for some time with colleagues to refine primary preventive measures by which health visitors can screen the general population for risk of child maltreatment (Browne and Saqi 1988; Browne and Herbert 1997). Significantly, predictive factors have included: parental history of family violence; single or separated parent; unemployment; history of mental illness, drug or alcohol addiction; and parent abused or neglected as a child. The only item not on Greenland's list is 'parent indifferent, intolerant or over-anxious towards child'.

Of the few attempts to compare fatal and non-fatal cases, Husain and Daniel (1984) compared filicidal and abusive mothers referred by courts for psychiatric assessment and concluded that the risk of fatality as a complication of child abuse increases significantly when mental illness is present in the mother. However, Alfaro (1988) collated the findings from nine studies in the United States and found that the only features which statistically distinguished between fatal and non-fatal cases were: child very young; child health problems; young mother; and male caretaker's history of criminality and drug use. Wilczynski (1995) also concluded that very few factors appear to be specific to filicide.

Although Greenland's list does offer a useful framework for assessment, it exemplifies the problem with risk checklists for the prediction of fatal abuse, which have been summarised by Wilczynski (1997):

- they are better at distinguishing between groups rather than individuals;
- they are over-inclusive and generate a high number of false positives;

- they are insufficiently sensitive and generate a high number of false negatives, especially since the problem is rare;
- they are based on imprecise studies, with inconsistent definitions of abuse, no control groups and unrepresentative samples;
- there is poor predictive clustering of factors and they do not adequately discriminate between non-fatal and fatal cases;
- there has been little attention to buffering factors;
- prior professional contact with the families has not usually focused on maltreatment.

Recognising the risk of serial filicide

Resnick (1970), Wilkins (1985) and McGrath (1992) have suggested that the repetition of infanticide is very rare indeed. However, it is now recognised that a small number of parents, predominantly mothers, kill successive children in ways that can go undetected. The children may be smothered and, in the absence of diagnostic post-mortem evidence, the death is recorded as SIDS (Emery 1985, 1986; Meadow 1990; d'Orban 1990; Hobbs *et al.* 1995; Hobbs and Wynne 1996). Other children are slowly poisoned or the parents induce symptoms such as fits and bring the child to paediatricians with illnesses that defy diagnostic efforts: the Munchausen syndrome-by-proxy (Meadow 1982, 1984). It is only if the physician becomes suspicious and investigates the circumstances further that it becomes apparent that the child was killed (Southall *et al.* 1987, 1997) and that previous siblings had also died in mysterious or suspicious circumstances, although their death had also been recorded at the time as SIDS.

This recognition that some abuse-related infant deaths are misdiagnosed as SIDS means that, if the cause of death had been more accurately determined, a similar fate to later siblings might have been avoided (Emery 1985). Meadow (1984) discussed 32 children whose parents presented them with fictitious epilepsy: they had a total of 33 siblings, 7 of whom had died suddenly and unexpectedly in infancy. Meadow (1990) later described 27 children whose deaths from suffocation were confirmed following recurrent symptoms of apnoea, cyanosis or seizures. Between them, they had had 33 siblings, 18 of whom had died suddenly in early life, often following similar episodes, and most had been diagnosed as SIDS. In 128 cases of Munchausen syndrome-by-proxy notified to a central register, 83 of the families had contained siblings, of whom 18 had previously died, 5 with a diagnosis of SIDS (McClure *et al.* 1996). Southall *et al.* (1997) detailed abuse to 39 children by their parents confirmed through covert video surveillance after they had been admitted to hospital with episodes of loss of consciousness, cyanosis or apnoea. These 39 children had 41 siblings, 12 of whom had died unexpectedly and a diagnosis of SIDS had been given to 11 of them. Four parents ultimately admitted suffocating 8 of these 12 siblings and a ninth was found to have died from deliberate salt poisoning.

Bacon (1997) has therefore advised that post-mortem pathologists should be more experienced at recognising the subtle signs of child abuse and should be provided with the social history of the child who has died as well as the medical history so that they could consider a wider range of causes of death. The training of more specialist paediatric pathologists is also advised. As we have discussed earlier, a particularly important impact of the Child Death Review Teams in the United Sates has been to heighten sensitivity amongst pathologists and coroners to the possibility of maltreatment causing children's death and to detect serial killings. We would hope that, if implemented, our recommendation for the establishment of local and regional standing committees to review all child deaths would reduce the likelihood of missed abuse cases and act as a preventive measure for siblings in the family.

Predictive inferences from our two studies

Although the main purpose of our two studies was not to identify predictive factors for fatal abuse, some of the processes we have described can contribute to our knowledge about preventive measures. However, it is important to acknowledge that their predictive potential remains to be validated in everyday practice. At this stage, they are best regarded as alerting features that, once recognised, point to the need for a more detailed assessment.

Closure

Closure was evident in over half of the 35 cases in the *Beyond Blame* study. It usually occurred in intermittent cycles and, by piecing together the chronology of events and medical evidence of the timing of the physical injuries to the child, it was evident that the episodes of closure had coincided with periods of escalating abuse. An episode of closure also tended to lead up to the death of the child, but this 'terminal closure' was no different in character from previous phases of intermittent closure. We inferred, therefore, that all periods of closure by families known to professionals because of a history of abuse should be considered an indicator of heightened risk to the child under surveillance that may prove fatal (Reder and Duncan 1995a, 1996).

A few other authors have also noted this phenomenon in abuse-related fatalities, including Oliver (1988), who termed it 'avoidance behaviour'. Greenland observed that 'failure to gain access to a previously abused child should be regarded as one of the most critical danger signals' (1987: 167–8). Armstrong and Wood reviewed nine infant deaths known to a Children's Hospital in Brisbane and found that: 'In all cases parents were avoidant of home visits and failed to attend appointments at other centres' (1991: 595).

Warnings

A number of the caretakers in both of our studies had approached professionals and communicated what was, in retrospect, a covert admission that abuse was critically escalating, for they were followed shortly afterwards by the child's death. Sometimes, these warnings were disguised as concern for the child's health or welfare or requests for their child to be looked after by the local authority. In other cases, the parents had revealed more overtly that they had thought of killing their child.

As we discussed more fully in Chapter 5, equivalent observations have been made by a number of other authors. For example, Bennie and Sclare (1969) reported that five of ten physically abusing parents had seen a doctor immediately preceding the assault, including to complain about the child's behaviour and to seek help in management. Three of the nine women interviewed by Korbin (1989) had either contacted a paediatrician or another family member a few days before they had fatally assaulted their child, including to express concerns about the child's safety.

Clearly, a vast number of parents ask social workers to take their child into care or complain to physicians about their child and it is only in retrospect that we have been able to claim that such parental behaviour was a covert warning of impending fatal abuse. However, these observations do point to the need for increased vigilance and suspiciousness by professionals. As with closure, in the context of a known history of child abuse by the parents, professionals should be aware that requests for care or displaced health inquiries about the child may signal escalating abuse that could prove fatal to a vulnerable child. The inference is that overt warnings should be taken seriously and that practitioners should be sensitive to the masked message that may be contained in apparently innocuous remarks. An additional clue from this present series of cases was that the anxiety of the parent or the pressure of their demand seemed out of keeping with the nature of the problem being presented. A typical example was the mother who telephoned the midwife one evening to insist that she must give up breast-feeding that night.

Serial filicide

As regards to repetition of fatal abuse, three of the thirty-five *Beyond Blame* cases involved parents who had killed or nearly killed a previous child and, of the thirty-five certain abuse fatalities in this follow-up study, there were five confirmations or strong suspicions that the perpetrator had previously killed another child, either of their own or whilst childminding. The significance of SIDS misdiagnoses for later siblings is underlined by two deaths which we reviewed during these projects. In both instances, misdiagnosis of a previous child's death meant that primary care professionals were visiting the family to try to prevent recurrence of SIDS. They had no reason to consider that there was a risk of fatal abuse with the next child and, as a result, were less sensitive than they might otherwise have been to evidence that the child was being mistreated. This underlines the importance of accurate histories as the basis for assessments.

Mental health problems

The link between fatal child abuse and caretakers' mental health problems found in this and other studies needs to be noted but also put into perspective. Most parents with psychiatric problems can and do provide good-enough care for their children. However, a small minority kill their child. As with all the other phenomena identified in our studies, the greatest significance of this is to alert practitioners to the risk so that they assess it more fully. Two particular clues have emerged from this review. The first is that parents in the midst of a psychiatric illness may make overt threats to harm their child: these warnings should be taken seriously. The second is that children of parents who are suffering from a psychotic illness are at considerable risk when incorporated into their parents' delusional thinking or hallucinations.

Risk assessment and the perinatal period

This study has helped us propose a model of risk, based upon appraisal of crises in the caretakers' unresolved care and/or control conflicts. While we do not claim that this model is reliably predictive of the risk of severe or fatal child abuse, we do believe that it has merits as a framework within which to conduct assessments. If the caretakers are known to have experienced abuse and rejection in childhood and their history of relationships with others suggests residues of unresolved care or control conflicts, including maltreatment of a child of their own, then episodes of crisis could be considered as especially risky to that child.

The perinatal period emerges from this review as the most relevant and opportune time to assess unresolved care and control conflicts and such links to the meaning of the child to its parent(s), as well as to target preventive resources towards the most vulnerable group of children. First, the very young ages of the children who were killed is consistent with numerous other studies. Many children were in the first weeks or months of life and therefore had recently been in contact with maternity services, even if fleetingly. Second, the implications of parental care–control conflicts and manifestation of the meaning of the child, both of which have significance for future risk, are potentially most available for assessment during the perinatal period. Two of the cases provide salutary illustrations.

One 16-year-old mother-to-be was booked for shared antenatal care with her GP but she received virtually no care because she moved frequently from home to home. When she was seen, a brief history would have revealed a young person who had experienced physical abuse from her father, two years in the care of the local authority and continuing strife with her mother. She had taken overdoses before becoming pregnant and another during the pregnancy, which had been conceived during a brief relationship with the child's father. She was discharged back to her own mother's home from the post-natal ward, despite her stepfather saying he refused to let her bring the baby into the house. Over the following weeks, this young mother tried to wean the baby on to solid food and declined to attend to the child's medical needs.[15]

Taken together, these themes suggest an adolescent still in conflict with her own mother, who found that her baby offered her a new opportunity to try to obtain the emotional care from her family that was previously missing. However, this was unforthcoming and she struggled alone with the dependency demands of a small baby that competed with her own unfulfilled need for care. Furthermore, recognition of such unresolved conflicts in one parent points to the importance of assessing *both* caretakers. This infant was killed by his father at the age of four months when temporarily left in his care.

> In another case, the mother's request for a termination of pregnancy could not be acceded to because the pregnancy was too advanced. The general practitioner presumed that his partner would provide ongoing support and was unaware that the mother failed to request any antenatal care, gave birth alone and let the newborn baby die from neglect of its basic needs.[26]

Brief enquiries about the meaning of the child-to-be could have revealed that the pregnancy had been conceived during an extra-marital affair and was unwanted.

Children who are 'unwanted' in some way are among those identified as at risk of maltreatment generally (Altemeier *et al.* 1984; Murphy *et al.* 1985) and of fatal abuse or neglect in particular (Resnick 1970; d'Orban 1979; Oliver 1983). This study has shown that clues to this in the perinatal period include the mother considering termination of the pregnancy, failing to present for antenatal care, wanting the baby to be adopted but changing her mind at the last moment, or carrying a baby conceived as the result of incestuous abuse.

There are numerous reports in the literature of perinatal screening procedures which have predictive potential. The most useful have been those which address social and interactional issues (e.g. Benedict *et al.* 1985; Starr 1988; Egan *et al.* 1990) rather than medical factors associated with the birth. Screening procedures, followed by home visiting programmes, have been demonstrated to be effective and efficient preventive measures by Olds *et al.* (1986, 1997), Hardy and Streett (1989) and Browne and Herbert (1997).

Browne (1989, 1995a) argues that, in order to be cost effective and to eliminate false alarms, screening for potential child abuse in the post-natal period should have at least three stages. All families with a newborn child should be screened for stressful social and demographic characteristics and all parents in the identified target group should be further screened three to six months later for their perceptions of the child and for family stresses. The infant's attachment to the primary caregiver and parental sensitivity to the infant's behaviour should be further assessed at nine to twelve months of age. Browne proposes that the secondary screening procedures should consider: the caretakers' knowledge of and attitudes to parenting; parental perceptions of the child's behaviour; parental emotions and responses to stress; parent–child interactions; and quality of child-to-parent attachments.

This present study has enabled us to confirm and highlight certain process factors which we believe are relevant to prediction of risk of future harm. They are:

- a parent's history of maltreatment, rejection and/or being in the care of the local authority as a child;
- an unresolved conflictual relationship with family-of-origin;
- a violent relationship between the parental couple;
- the presence of a mental health problem in either parent, especially substance misuse and delusional thinking involving the child;
- minimal antenatal care;
- ambivalence about, or rejection of, the pregnancy;
- the child being attributed with a negative meaning.

This is not intended as a list of risk indicators, but as a series of scenarios which should alert practitioners to undertake more detailed assessment. They need to be validated in more systematic research, but, in the meantime, we are struck by the similarity between these suggested pointers and those described by others. For instance, the Family Stress Checklist utilised by Murphy *et al.* (1985) included equivalent themes, as did the protocols used by Soumenkoff *et al.* (1982) and Egan *et al.* (1990). Bonnet (1993) and Finnegan *et al.* (1982) have discussed similar issues in the assessment of mothers who have denied awareness of their pregnancy, while Kelley (1992) emphasises the association between intrauterine exposure to drugs and subsequent child maltreatment.

In our view, there is merit in antenatal clinic staff, and/or GPs, taking a brief history that elicits the interactional factors that have been identified. This need not be an elaborate interview, but opportunities should be found to ask mothers-to-be about their attitude to the pregnancy, their own history of being parented, their relationship with the child's father and their practical plans for looking after the baby. If they had first wanted the baby to be adopted and then changed their mind, the reasons behind this ambivalence need to be assessed and the implications considered. Ideally, equivalent interviews should be held with the biological or non-biological father in the household.

The post-natal period provides further opportunities for considering these issues, as well as for identifying post-natal depression or psychosis. During the early months of a child's life, health visitors have a crucial role observing their physical and emotional welfare and the development of parent–child relationships. As Browne and others have shown, they are ideally placed to undertake preliminary screening assessments in order to identify vulnerable families who would benefit from targeted preventive services. In our view, continued investment in this primary care role could play a major part in the future protection of those children at greatest risk of harm. Resources could also usefully be directed towards further training of midwives and health visitors in order to develop their assessment skills in this area.

Synthesis

Most commentators conclude that it is not possible to predict accurately which parent will kill their child. According to the US Advisory Board on Child Abuse and Neglect:

> Research suggests that the same kinds of high risk family situations are producing both fatally and seriously injured children … If true, prevention efforts directed at the larger group of families with the potential to seriously injure their children will encompass the smaller group of families at risk for fatalities. With the right approach, we also may be able to prevent so-called 'serial' fatal abuse and neglect by parents who have already lost one child but remain undetected by the system because the death was diagnosed as accidental or natural.
>
> (1995: 128)

Wilczynski also reported that: 'identifying a potential child-killer from a caseload of at-risk parents is a very difficult task. Indeed, there is general agreement that the only effective way to prevent child fatalities is to improve service provision to the entire at-risk population' (1997: 197). Alfaro (1988: 257) concluded that: 'the demand for accurate prediction is unrealistic in view of the nature of the fatality phenomenon and problems in predicting human behaviour in general', while Levine *et al.* (1994) believed that: 'the difference between a fatal

and nonfatal injury may be a matter of chance. The conditions trig-
gering severe injury or fatality are probably highly similar' (p. 456)
and: 'No risk measure is so closely predictive of actual harm that it
could be used to justify drastic legal intervention into families' (p. 465).

If our predictive capacities are meagre, is it appropriate to focus
research or practice resources on the very rare fatal child abuse event?
This is partially a moral issue, since one measure of society's concern
for its citizens is its willingness to focus on childhood and on children's
suffering. Another dimension is the estimate offered by Baladerian
(quoted by the US Advisory Board on Child Abuse and Neglect 1995)
that at least ten times as many children survive abuse as die from it and
are left permanently and severely disabled. In the UK, Buchanan and
Oliver (1977) found that the brain damage of at least 3 per cent, and
possibly up to 11 per cent, of children residing in 'subnormality' hospitals had been directly caused by violent abuse or neglect.

The question has been raised whether preoccupation with
predicting and preventing fatalities has inappropriately skewed practitioners' efforts. Gibbons *et al.* noted during their follow-up study of
abused children that:

> The unstated fear behind the [child protection] procedures may be
> that another child will be killed. Yet this is a comparatively rare
> event that can probably never be successfully predicted ... The
> ever-present fear of serious or fatal injury to a child may explain
> why the social workers in this study concentrated on surveillance
> and monitoring to ensure children's physical safety. They appeared
> to pay less attention to warning signs of distorted socio-emotional
> development and low achievement.
>
> (1995: 176)

The Department of Health (1995) went on to encourage local
authorities to review the balance of their work between statutory
investigation and family support. The sad irony is that the social
workers censured by the Jasmine Beckford inquiry had been focusing
their endeavours on supporting the parents. The key issues must be
that an appropriate *balance* needs to be struck between statutory intervention and support and that this balance should be reviewed
continually. We believe that approaches to practice guided by a
dialectic mindset are most likely to promote such a self-reflective
stance.

It seems unrealistic to expect that all child deaths at the hands of
their caretakers can be predicted and prevented. Unfortunately, abuse

fatalities will continue to occur. However, it is apparent that there are different pathways leading to fatal abuse which epidemiological research does not satisfactorily distinguish. Clinical case studies, on the other hand, have the potential to alert professionals to constellations of factors which, taken together, could enhance prediction of serious maltreatment or fatal abuse. A greater understanding of seriously abusive scenarios might help reduce the number of such tragedies.

Practice issues

- The realistic aim of preventive measures should be to *reduce* the incidence of severe or fatal child abuse.
- Improved recognition of which child abuse deaths are misdiagnosed as SIDS would reduce the risk of serial filicide.
- Assessment by midwives and health visitors in the perinatal period could promote the identification of vulnerable families and allow services to be targeted towards them in order to reduce the risks of serious injury to children.
- Prevention could be improved by the recognition of episodes of closure, covert warnings, parental delusional thinking incorporating the child, and manifestations of unresolved care and control conflicts.

8 Facilitating good practice

This has been a detailed study of 49 fatal child abuse and neglect cases, involving the deaths of 51 children. The 'Part 8' Review files allowed us to consider child protection practice at a number of different levels, including national collation of epidemiological data, the functioning of local child protection networks and risk evaluation as part of day-to-day case management. The study followed up a previous review of 35 cases that had been subject to public inquiry, so that, overall, we have been able to reanalyse the circumstances of 86 child maltreatment fatalities and draw additional practice lessons from them.

An interactional perspective enabled us to identify significant relationship patterns in the caretakers' lives, within the children's families and within the professional networks, that added new meaning to the demographic and factual features of the cases. We noted a number of factors that affected the outcome of the cases and many of the practice implications revolved around the way that professionals processed information and approached assessments. We had particular concerns about practitioners failing to obtain background information, treating information discretely so that a threshold of concern was not reached, intervening without the guide of an assessment and missing warning signs.

So far, we have separated out each factor in order to describe it and to identify common themes across the cases. In this final chapter, we shall draw these various threads together through a general discussion about the genesis of tragedies and suggest how the risks could be reduced. These principles will then be translated into the ethos that we believe should underpin everyday professional practice and, therefore, the training of those who will contribute to child protection networks.

Learning from tragedies

Service delivery is not merely a matter of avoiding disasters but, since professional practice is based on a covert preparedness for a worst-case scenario, it is possible to use an understanding of tragedies as a guide to good practice.

One process phenomenon that might help us further understand what goes wrong when a child dies is contained in a notion of 'cumulative error'. This describes how single factors, that would in themselves be relatively harmless, interact and compound each other so that the risk of a disaster is greatly multiplied. If each factor is at a marginal level of safety, the cumulative nature of a series of marginal risks will occasionally produce a runaway effect, precipitating an overwhelming catastrophe.

Examples of this phenomenon commonly cited outside the realm of child protection are the floundering of the ferry *Herald of Free Enterprise* near Zeebrugge harbour in 1987 with the loss of almost 200 lives (Crainer 1993) and the Hillsborough football stadium disaster in 1989, when nearly one hundred football spectators were crushed to death (Taylor 1989).

The ferry turned over following a sudden influx of sea water through bow doors that had been left open when the vessel set sail. However, subsequent inquiries revealed that a series of boardroom decisions about design costs, load limits, reduced turn-round times and rest periods, and so on, had significantly decreased the safety margins of the whole service. Each change had, in itself, been acceptably safe but none had been considered within the context of all the other marginally safe changes that had taken place. The series of decisions had interacted to generate wider margins of error over time, increasing the risk of a final massive catastrophe. The company's management board should have considered the likely consequences of each specific decision about the service in the context of the possible impact of all previous decisions.

The precipitant of the Hillsborough disaster was a sudden surge of fans on to the terraces, crushing those ahead of them, after a large exit gate was opened by the police to allow supporters to enter the ground. However, the contexts for this event included recent invasions of pitches by football followers which had led the authorities to erect insurmountable barriers around all enclosures, many supporters arriving for the game close to kick-off time, tickets for the match having been distributed so that the club with larger support was allocated the smaller end of the ground, police deciding to open the gate to relieve a dangerous crush in the approaches to turnstiles at that end, and inadequate arrangements to direct fans to different terracing enclosures inside the stadium. It is possible that each factor in itself might have been manageable, but together they interacted to produce a major tragedy.

Translating back to the area of child protection, we can speculate that a single event, such as a failure to assess or a missed warning sign, would not necessarily constitute a fatal error. However, with certain families, continuing to plan strategies that have not been guided by any assessment would multiply the risk exponentially and significantly heighten the risk of severe harm. Over our two studies, we identified a number of processes that affected child protection practice and individual cases usually contained more than one of these processes. If each factor, itself of marginal significance in terms of practice error, interacted and produced a major deviation from safe practice, how could this be handled in order to minimise the dangers to children? In our view, the solution is twofold.

First, it is necessary to address carefully each facet of practice so that it does not have the opportunity to compound problems in other areas and contribute to a runaway catastrophe. Each decision or intervention needs to be thought through and the reasoning behind it made explicit. The possible risks should be considered and the advantages and disadvantages balanced. The likely impact of the planned intervention on the family and on the work of other involved practitioners should be appreciated and, once implemented, the actual impact must be monitored. This may sound like an unnecessarily laborious exercise and unrealistic as an approach to *every* piece of practice. However, we are suggesting that this should be an automatic way of thinking that underpins all work and takes only moments each time.

Second, it is essential to consider each element of practice in context. In other words, decisions should be taken in the light of what is known about past interventions and their impact, as well as current inputs from others and their effectiveness. Once again, if this becomes automatic thinking, then it takes very little time to implement. It involves a degree of self-reflection and a readiness to consider the importance of interaction and feedback.

In fact, what we are recommending is a way of thinking that we have referred to as a dialectic mindset. In Chapter 5, we discussed the benefits of undertaking assessments within this mindset. We can now develop this argument beyond the assessment process and suggest that it is relevant to every aspect of day-to-day practice. The mindset opens up practitioners' thinking so that they place current information in its wider context and consider alternative ways to explain observations. It encourages them to recognise feedback mechanisms and to appreciate that every action has a reaction. Most particularly, it emphasises the continual interplay between thought and action.

This way of thinking should be acquired during training and reinforced through continuing professional development of qualified practitioners. We shall therefore go on to a fuller discussion of professional training and then consider how the same principles apply to post-qualifying experiences and working practices.

Professional training

Even though the pre-qualifying courses of the various professions will contain different areas of knowledge, theoretical premises and practical skills, we believe that a dialectic mindset is a way of thinking that should be acquired by all practitioners. It should be central to the work of all members of child protection networks and therefore applies across professional boundaries.

An ethos for training

The same diagram that we used to summarise the assessment process can be used to illustrate the necessary elements of training – see Figure 8.1. Trainees need to become familiar with a body of knowledge relevant to their profession but they should also be encouraged to think about it, to question it and to seek out additional information that complements or challenges it. They should become curious about ideas and be able to debate the supporting and counter-arguments. They should become conversant with theoretical frameworks that help them organise the knowledge they acquire and help them consider it critically. The literature containing theory, research and practice experiences should be referred to repeatedly and respected as a source to satisfy inquiry. The methodology contained in research papers should also be used to help trainees develop hypotheses, pose questions, seek alternative explanations and then draw inferences. They should be taught specific practice skills, together with criteria that guide the application of such interventions and the monitoring of their outcome. The thinking and practical elements should be shown to be complementary, so that, for example, intervention skills are understood within a theoretical framework.

All this should come together in professional training that facilitates thinking as well as doing and teaches both in depth and in breadth. In

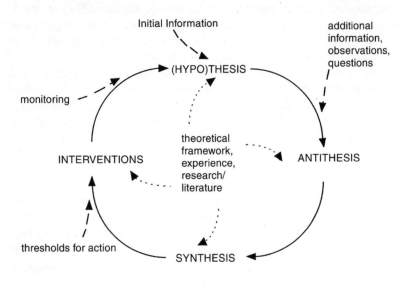

Figure 8.1   The 'dialectic' mindset as a guide to professional training

other words, trainees should be offered an 'education' that includes a grounding in academic principles and intelligent application of a repertoire of practical skills. The courses must be of sufficient length to allow trainees to explore and rehearse the theory and practice elements and appreciate their interrelationship. Discussions about how this might apply to social work and psychiatry, for example, can be found in Webb (1996), Jones (1996) and Reder *et al.* (in press).

Training for professionalism

Training programmes should aim to lay a secure foundation for professionalism in future practice. Cruess and Cruess (1997) have summarised the core characteristics of a profession, which include: commanding a discrete body of knowledge and skills; being governed by a code of ethics; being granted the right to self-regulation through mandated associations which organise, formalise and monitor practice independent of the state and the member's workplace and are responsible for the ethical and technical criteria by which their members are evaluated; and admission being through a prolonged period of education and training. In addition, professionals' knowledge and skills are expected to be used to provide a service to the public and autonomy is given on the understanding that the welfare of those seeking their services and of society in general will be prioritised.

It is our opinion that the training of all key members of child protection networks should prepare them for a future role as professionals and not simply as practitioners with specific technical competencies. The need to maintain high ethical and practical standards, to think through a case at different levels and to arrive at informed and independent judgements are all essential requirements of this work and these qualities only truly reside in professionalism.

An example of the difference independence makes can be found in approaches to assessment. Some practitioners are instructed that they should only recommend interventions that are within the known resources available to their agency and therefore their assessments start with the premise that certain conclusions would be unacceptable. While it makes logical sense to tailor intervention strategies to the facilities available to carry them out, independent professionals would approach the issue in a different way. They start their assessment neutral to the likely outcome and base their recommendations about the ideal intervention on their assessment material. Only then do they address the question of what resources are available to meet those needs and, if there is a discrepancy between the identified needs and the resources, this is highlighted.

Translating ethos into content

Having suggested a core ethos for training, we shall consider examples of how this might be translated into the contents of pre-qualifying training schemes and continuing professional development after qualification. Once again, it is evident that specific professions will acquire their own knowledge base and practice skills. However, we believe that there are certain areas that should be considered relevant to all the professions who will work with children and families and who will become involved in child protection work. These particularly concern learning about: interactional processes; the functioning of individuals within their social and relational contexts; family relationships; children's development; collating together complex information from diverse sources; and interprofessional communication.

In order to illustrate how some of these topics can be addressed, we shall mention examples with which we are familiar. A fuller discussion of training exercises can be found in works by Watzlawick *et al.* (1974), Whiffen and Byng-Hall (1982), Burnham (1986), Stratton *et al.* (1990), Smith (1993) and Reder (1996c), among others.

Learning to think 'interaction' and 'family'

A core axiom for those entering the helping professions should be that the people they will be assessing and treating live in relationship with others and their problems often arise in the context of these relationships. While psychodynamic, behavioural and cognitive models contribute significantly to the understanding of individual functioning, we believe that they need to be brought together and integrated through an interactional framework. Appreciating the importance of interactional contexts also enables practitioners to reflect on their own functioning within their work setting and within networks of other professionals. Hence, an interactional theme, including theories of systemic and group processes, could usefully run through all training programmes.

For instance, child development can be explained as an interplay between intrapsychic and interactional processes. Observation of infants in their home setting has long been a feature of psychotherapy training (e.g. Reid 1997) and is being introduced into the experiences of other professionals, such as child psychiatrists (e.g. Etchegoyen and Stubley 1997). The trainee visits a young family weekly over months or years in order to observe the child's everyday behaviour. Detailed notes of the hour-long observations are discussed with a tutor, focusing on the infant's behaviour in relation to others. Hypotheses are developed about the infant's developmental progress, inner world, impact on others and reaction to them, and so on.

Modified forms of this programme can be evolved, tailoring them to the needs of the trainees. A variation would be for trainees to observe a family containing slightly older children. However, family interaction can be complex and a useful introduction is to watch video tapes, prepared either using actors simulating a family or scenes from commercial films, in order to note individuals' verbal and non-verbal communication. Afterwards, the group can discuss with the tutor what they observed and collate the patterns of interaction that were portrayed. This 'micro-analysis' of interaction is an invaluable aid to the learning of observation skills and developing hypotheses about relationships.

As a result of the early specialisation which now occurs in professional careers, especially separating those who address children's problems from those who are concerned with adults, practitioners tend to be relatively uninformed about the other age groups. The association between fatal child abuse and adult mental health problems identified in this and related studies reinforces the need for practitioners to be able to consider problems from the perspectives of children *and* adults, together with their mutual interaction. The principal training orientation of many adult mental health service workers is on their patients as individuals, with only secondary regard for them as participants in interacting family units, each member of whom has an impact on the others. The greater sharing of knowledge between adult and child mental health services should start during undergraduate training and continue in later professional practice, through regular teaching events which address issues across the age barrier (Reder *et al.*, in press). In addition, training in, and experience of, conjoint family therapy approaches could help widen the thinking of all practitioners so that it becomes automatic to take account of the experiences of other family members and to consider their interrelationships.

Learning to collate information and ask: 'What don't I know?'

Much of the discussion on assessment in Chapter 5 and on training in this chapter has emphasised the thinking that helps practitioners to organise information that *is* available to them. However, the synthesis that arises out of this organisation should also act as a guide to the information that remains unknown, the gaps in knowledge that would allow a fuller understanding of the family and their problems and professional responses to them. In Figure 8.1, it is the 'additional information, observations and questions' arc that leads to 'antithesis' and eventually to a 'synthesis'.

The genogram offers a good illustration of this, since it is a structure that both organises details about a family's history and composition (see McGoldrick and Gerson 1985) and also highlights areas of missing information. Figure 8.2 is an example, using the genogram of Maria Colwell, whose death at the hands of her stepfather represented a watershed in the history of child protection in the UK (Inquiry Report 1974; Reder *et al.* 1993a).

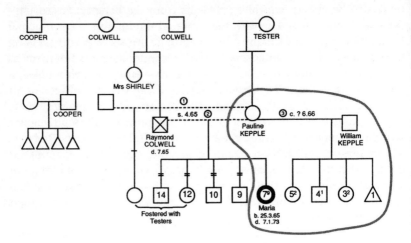

Figure 8.2 Genogram of Maria Colwell's family
Source: Reder *et al.* 1993a

The diagram shows that the mother, Pauline Kepple, had ten children from three different partners. The first daughter was from an unmarried relationship, and this child was fostered from birth. Maria was the youngest of five children born to Pauline Kepple's relationship with Raymond Colwell and she was born in March 1965. Her parents separated in April 1965 and her father died in July. Four of Maria's elder siblings were taken into care soon afterwards. Pauline Kepple went on to cohabit with William Kepple around June 1966 and then to marry him. They had four children, although the sex of the youngest was not reported and is depicted by a triangle symbol. The household at the time of Maria's death in January 1973 is enclosed within the stippled line and the ages of the other children at that time ranged from 5 years to 1 year. Minimal information was reported about the background of Pauline Kepple and none at all about William Kepple. Mr Cooper was a half-brother to Raymond Colwell and he and his wife had four children whose sex was not recorded. Maria was fostered into that family for six years before being returned to live in her mother's new family.

A great deal of information is summarised in this genogram, but it is evident that there is virtually no information about the parental figures and their personal backgrounds. In particular, the background of William Kepple, the stepfather who killed Maria, was not given in the inquiry report and so it is impossible to speculate on his psychological functioning and relationships with others.

This case also illustrates how the structural drawing of the genogram acts as the basis for organising information about the history of relationships between family members and then allows hypotheses to be developed about repetitive patterns, together with the areas of unknown information that might need to be discovered, such as at interview. Maria is usually remembered as the 7-year-old child who was killed after she was removed from a foster home, where she was thriving, and forced to live with her natural mother and stepfather because of the importance given at the time to the so-called 'blood-tie'. However, carefully piecing together the family history suggests that the meaning of Maria to her mother was probably unwittingly an important contribution to the decision to return Maria to her (Reder *et al.* 1993; Reder and Duncan 1995b). We shall repeat the history shown on the genogram, adding further information about the fluctuations in relationships over time.

Pauline Kepple's first child was from an unmarried liaison and she placed her with the maternal grandmother from birth. The father of Pauline's next five children was Raymond Colwell and Maria was the youngest of that family. Raymond left the household one month after Maria's birth and he died three months later. Pauline Kepple soon became depressed and neglectful of all her children. However, she treated Maria differently from the others and, just a few weeks after Raymond Colwell's death, she decided to take Maria to the Coopers, who agreed to look after her. Eventually, the remaining children were taken into care because of neglect and two were also placed with their maternal grandmother. However, Maria was the only one of the children with whom Pauline Kepple kept in contact and the only one of her absent children whom she insisted remain Catholic, like herself. Over the next six years, Pauline Kepple made a number of requests for Maria to return to her, always at times of transition in her own life. These attempts to be reunited with Maria occurred when the mother was planning to settle down with, and then marry, William Kepple, and again when she became pregnant by him. She made yet another request to have Maria back when her youngest baby was 3-months-old, the age Maria had been when she gave her up. Maria was eventually returned when she was 6-years-old and she was neglected, assaulted and rejected over the next year until dying from violent abuse by William Kepple.

This story suggested to us that Maria had a special meaning to her mother because her birth was associated with the loss of Raymond Colwell. Pauline Kepple was then unable to let Maria go as she had done the other children, clinging on to the memory of the 3-month-old baby and wanting to be reunited with her as a way of dealing with her unresolved feelings about the loss of Raymond Colwell. However, Maria's actual identity when she did return must have contrasted dramatically with the fantasised meaning that predominated in her mother's mind. She was not the baby who might help her mother resolve the loss of the father, but a 7-year-old who was upset and regressed after being displaced from her foster home and who continued to reject her new caretakers in preference for her old ones. The missing information about William Kepple prevents us speculating on the meaning of Maria to him, beyond, perhaps, the possibility of being a reminder to him that his wife had once had an intimate relationship with another man.

Familiarity with genograms, therefore, would enhance the training of all those entering the helping professions. Compiling case chronologies is another core skill to be imparted during training. It is a complementary means of integrating together known information so that an overview of 'the case as a whole' emerges and of helping the practitioner identify missing details that need to be sought. Figure 1.4 in the opening chapter is a guide to mapping the history of a child protection case that can be used for training. As the account of events unfolds, the practitioner learns to keep asking: *What happened next?* and *What else do I need to know about that event?*. For instance, if a child protection conference was reported to be held, the practitioner also needs to know: *What was the reason for calling it? Who attended? What were the conclusions? What child protection plans emerged from it? Were they implemented? With what effect?* And so on.

Learning about communication

Problems with communication were a major finding from the *Beyond Blame* project, although they did not emerge so clearly from the present study. Perhaps this was because large networks of professionals had not been involved over such long periods in the more recent group. However, it is probably reasonable to presume that some of the assessment problems, especially thresholds of concern not reaching a critical level, were attributable to communication difficulties. Certainly, there is continual evidence from everyday practice that the learning of communication skills needs to be improved.

The same principles that underlie assessment also apply to communication, since it requires a mindset which acknowledges that thought and action are interrelated. The activities of speaking, writing and listening will remain unproductive unless their contents are thought about, organised and rendered clear by the message sender and the possible meanings considered by the receiver. Each participant in the dialogue should be able to monitor their style of communication and be aware of its possible impact on the other person. For example: *Have they understood what I intended to convey? Do they appreciate my level of concern? Have I distinguished the important information from the incidental?* and *Do we agree who will do what following our exchange of information?* All these components of communication can be taught through observation, modelling, role play and rehearsal.

Post-qualifying practice

The learning process started in pre-qualifying courses should be sustained afterwards through continuing professional development. This includes support for practitioners to attend advanced courses and conferences, encouragement to continue reading relevant literature and provision of personal supervision. However, none of these can occur unless the agency pays close attention to the working environment of its staff.

Concern about working contexts was a major theme to emerge from the *Beyond Blame* study, especially as it related to staffing levels within front-line agencies and the adequacy of resources to support those staff in post. The 'Part 8' Review reports that we read for this present study made little reference to this issue, concentrating instead on details of the cases. However, the last decade has witnessed significant restrictions to the funding of social services, the police, health services, and other elements of the child protection network. While adequacy of training helps make optimal use of resources that are available, no amount of training can compensate for inadequate staffing levels.

Indeed, Smith (1993) has warned that improved training, however important, does not replace the need also to provide adequate resources for the task practitioners are being trained to perform. Smith noted that many inquiry reports into fatal child abuse cases have recommended improvements in training, but she also observed that the solution to inadequate services cannot be a concentration on training without a concomitant investment in resources, otherwise this concentration inadvertently undermines the very training that has been provided.

Given appropriate resources, other facets of professionals' working contexts can usefully be considered as the application of a dialectic mindset, since this ethos is more than just a way of approaching discrete elements of training and practice. A good example comes from the use of procedural guidelines in everyday practice. As many of the original reviewers of the 'Part 8' cases emphasised, it is important for practitioners to follow the procedures that have been drawn up by central government, the local ACPC and their own agency. These procedures provide a set of parameters for activities and a structure for the work. However, in order to apply them effectively, staff need to understand the rationale behind them and think about their meaning for the particular case under consideration. Some procedures provide general guidance on good practice, some have significance for one set of circumstances but not for another, while some are essential rules to be followed universally. At a different level, monitoring the value of all procedures might reveal that some require clarification modification, or even deletion.

Similarly, good inter-agency liaison and communication are not processes that can be prescribed through procedural rules, since they are more a function of interpersonal relationships than organisational structures. Individual staff, as well as professional networks, need to review regularly their communication and liaison styles and find opportunities to make improvements. Such thinking and learning must be supported by the ethos of the workplace and this is often demonstrated by the way supervision and audit are approached.

It is surprising that few professions regard supervision of trainees or junior staff as an advanced skill that needs to be learned and refined. Some comments have already been made about supervision in Chapter 5, and it is clear that it should be seen as an opportunity for thinking and education and not just a mechanical exercise of deciding what to do with the practitioner's caseload. Areas of the supervisee's work and experience that need to be enhanced can be identified *by both parties* at the outset and cases selected for more detailed discussion because this would advance the practitioner's learning, overcome their blind spots or challenge fixed beliefs. Supervision meetings could allow, for example, details of family interviews to be presented and analysed, hypotheses developed and useful literature identified for later reading. The atmosphere needs to be containing enough to allow supervisees to consider a range of possible decisions available to them on particular cases and also to facilitate occasional reflection on the emotional impact the families have on them.

Supervision could address enhancing practitioners' communication skills in a number of ways. The practitioner could attend a child protection conference as observer in order to monitor its process as well as its content (Reder and Duncan 1990). They might decide to note how members contributed to the group dynamics, how they presented their information and opinions and critical points in the chair's guidance of the meeting. These observations may then be discussed in the next supervision session, with hypotheses developed about the group process and alternatives considered for how the trainee would have behaved if they had had a responsible role in the conference. When the time comes for the practitioner to contribute in reality to a conference, or to present evidence in court, rehearsal during supervision can significantly assist their competence.

Audit is another valuable aid to learning. We are not using the term 'audit' here in the sense of counting throughput of work, but the analysis of single cases in order to elicit practice lessons, in much the same way as we approached our two studies. An ideal training forum can be created by bringing together a multidisciplinary group in which details of a case are presented, with regular pauses to consider particular themes. These need to be identified at the outset and can focus on diverse aspects of practice. For example: *What understanding did the practitioners have of the information available to them? What group process may have propelled the child protection conference in the direction it took? Why did practitioners' threshold of concern reach a critical level at a particular point? Were local procedures observed?* Audit conducted in this way can be used to consider examples of good practice as well as problems.

In summary, then, we are suggesting that a dialectic mindset should underpin the training of professionals and should pervade the ethos of their workplace. It should provide containment for the complex tasks that they undertake and provide a framework that guides practice. In a sense, a metaphor for good professional practice is that it is a continuous process of assessment.

Finally, we would add a comment about how our two books – *Beyond Blame* and this present one – could be used to aid training. Both works have described an approach to collating information about complex cases, which then allows processes within and between members of the family and the network to emerge. The processes could be regarded as clues to assist hypothesising, so that a workshop might audit a case and pause regularly to consider how to understand its development, including what essential information is still missing from the picture (Jane Wonnacott, personal communication). From a training perspective, then, they could be used as an aid to thinking, so that our child protection practice continues to develop in both a thoughtful and an effective way.

Addendum

In September 1998, a few days before we were due to submit the manuscript of this book to the publishers, the Bridge Child Care Development Service launched its BridgeALERT pack for assessing risk of harm to children (Dent 1998). This was too late for us to integrate references to it into earlier sections of the book but we believe it is appropriate to mention it here, as an addendum to this chapter on applying the dialectic mindset, because it appears to be a valuable example of this way of thinking.

The assessment protocol consists of a series of questions for practitioners to answer, which collate information about the child, the caretakers and their social circumstances, and it is accompanied by a training manual. The questions are based on risk factors identified in the research literature (Hagell 1998) and the intention is to ensure that appropriate information is gathered together and understood within an explicit theoretical framework, and that crucial information which is unknown can be identified and sought. Many questions have a relational bias, such as exploring the caretaker's personal history and their interactions with professionals. The protocol is presented as a series of questions or prompts and their overall effect is to be an invitation to thinking as well as doing. The underlying theoretical model is presented in the opening pages of the schedule and each question is accompanied by an explanation that suggests how the answers may be understood. Wider exploration is encouraged by prompts about gathering together background information from the agency's files and from other involved professionals, while invitations to the assessor to be self-reflective include questions about how they are approaching the task and how they will monitor the outcome of their interventions.

The assessment pack has been piloted, but, at the time of writing, remains to be validated in a more systematic way. However, as an application of the way of thinking that we have endeavoured to describe in this book and a means of translating this mindset into a practical way forward, it seems to have much merit. We believe that it also provides pointers to future research projects that will have practical application in this challenging and complex area.

References

Agathonos-Georgopoulou, H. and Browne, K.D. (1997) 'The prediction of child maltreatment in Greek families', *Child Abuse and Neglect* 21: 721–35.

Ainsworth, M. (1982) 'Attachment: retrospect and prospect', in C. Murray Parkes and J. Stevenson-Hinde (eds) *The Place of Attachment in Human Behaviour*, London: Tavistock.

Alexander, R., Crabbe, L., Sato, Y., Smith, W. and Bennett, T. (1990) 'Serial abuse in children who are shaken', *American Journal of Disease of Children* 144: 58–60.

Alfaro, J. (1988) 'What can we learn from child abuse fatalities? A synthesis of nine studies', in D.J. Besharov (ed.) *Protecting Children from Abuse and Neglect: Policy and Practice*, Springfield, Ill.: Charles C. Thomas.

Altemeier, W.A., O'Connor, S., Vietze, P., Sandler, H. and Sherrod, K. (1984) 'Prediction of child abuse: a prospective study of feasibility', *Child Abuse and Neglect* 8: 393–400.

American Association for Protecting Children (1986) *Highlights of Official Child Neglect and Abuse Reporting: 1984*, Denver, Col.: American Humane Association.

Anderson, C.L. (1987) 'Assessing parenting potential for child abuse risk', *Pediatric Nursing* 13: 323–7.

Anderson, R., Ambrosino, R., Valentine, D. and Lauderdale, M. (1983) 'Child deaths attributed to abuse and neglect: an empirical study', *Child and Youth Services Review* 5: 75–89.

Anthony, E.J. and Kreitman, N. (1970) 'Murderous obsessions in mothers toward their children', in E.J. Anthony and T. Benedek (eds) *Parenthood: Its Psychology and Psychopathology*, Boston: Little, Brown.

Armstrong, K.L. and Wood, D. (1991) 'Can infant death from abuse be prevented?', *Medical Journal of Australia* 155: 593–6.

Bacon, C.J. (1997) 'Cot death after CESDI', *Archives of Disease in Childhood* 76: 171–3.

Bays, J. (1990) 'Substance abuse and child abuse: impact of addiction on the child', *Pediatric Clinics of North America* 37: 881–904.

Benedict, M.I., White, R.B. and Cornely, D.A. (1985) 'Maternal perinatal risk factors and child abuse', *Child Abuse and Neglect* 9: 217–24.

Bennie, E.H. and Sclare, A.B. (1969) 'The battered child syndrome', *American Journal of Psychiatry* 125: 147–51.

Black, R. and Mayer, J. (1980) 'Parents with special problems: alcohol and opiate addiction', in C.H. Kempe and R.E. Helfer (eds) *The Battered Child*, 3rd edn, Chicago: University of Chicago Press.

Bonnet, C. (1993) 'Adoption at birth: prevention against abandonment or neonaticide', *Child Abuse and Neglect* 17: 501–13.

Boscolo, L., Cecchin, G., Hoffman, L. and Penn, P. (1987) *Milan Systemic Family Therapy: Conversations in Theory and Practice*, New York: Basic Books.

Bourget, D. and Bradford, J.M.W. (1990) 'Homicidal parents', *Canadian Journal of Psychiatry* 35: 233–8.

Bowlby, J. (1969: 1973: 1980) *Attachment and Loss*, vols I–III, London: Hogarth.

—— (1977) 'The making and breaking of affectional bonds. I: Aetiology and psychopathology in the light of attachment theory', *British Journal of Psychiatry* 130: 201–10.

—— (1988) *A Secure Base: Clinical Applications of Attachment Theory*, London: Routledge.

Brewster, A.L., Nelson, J.P., Hymel, K.P., Colby, D.R., Lucas, D.R., McCanne, T.R. and Milner, J.S. (1998) 'Victim, perpetrator, family, and incident characteristics of 32 infant maltreatment deaths in the United States Air Force', *Child Abuse and Neglect* 22: 91–101.

Browne, D.H. (1986) 'The role of stress in the commission of subsequent acts of child abuse and neglect', *Journal of Family Violence* 1: 289–97.

Browne, K. (1989) 'The health visitor's role in screening for child abuse', *Health Visitor* 62: 275–7.

Browne, K. (1995a) 'Preventing child maltreatment through community nursing', *Journal of Advanced Nursing* 21: 57–63.

—— (1995b) 'Predicting maltreatment', in P. Reder and C. Lucey (eds) *Assessment of Parenting: Psychiatric and Psychological Contributions*, London: Routledge.

Browne, K. and Herbert, M. (1997) *Preventing Family Violence*, Chichester: Wiley.

Browne, K.D. and Lynch, M. (1995) 'The nature and extent of child homicide and fatal abuse', *Child Abuse Review* 4: 309–16.

Browne, K. and Saqi, S. (1988) 'Approaches to screening for child abuse and neglect', in K. Browne, C. Davies and P. Stratton (eds) *Early Prediction and Prevention of Child Abuse*, Chichester: Wiley.

Browne, K., Hanks, H. and Stratton, P. (eds) (2000) *The Prediction and Prevention of Child Abuse: A Handbook*, Chichester: Wiley.

Brozovsky, M. and Falit, H. (1971) 'Neonaticide: clinical and psychodynamic considerations', *Journal of the American Academy of Child Psychiatry* 10: 673–83.

Buchanan, A. and Oliver, J.E. (1977) 'Abuse and neglect as a cause of mental retardation: a study of 140 children admitted to subnormality hospitals in Wiltshire', *British Journal of Psychiatry* 131: 458–67.

Burnham, J. (1986) *Family Therapy: First Steps towards a Systemic Approach*, London: Tavistock.

Burns, E.C., O'Driscoll, M. and Wasson, G. (1996) 'The health and development of children whose mothers are on methadone maintenance', *Child Abuse Review* 5: 113–22.

Button, J.H. and Reivich, R.S. (1972) 'Obsessions of infanticide: a review of 42 cases', *Archives of General Psychiatry* 27: 235–40.

Campion, J.F., Cravens, J.M. and Covan, F. (1988) 'A study of filicidal men', *American Journal of Psychiatry* 145: 1141–4.

Carter, B. and McGoldrick, M. (eds) (1989) *The Changing Family Life Cycle: A Framework for Family Therapy*, 2nd edn, Boston: Allyn and Bacon.

Cassell, D. and Coleman, R. (1995) 'Parents with psychiatric problems', in P. Reder and C. Lucey (eds) *Assessment of Parenting: Psychiatric and Psychological Contributions*, London: Routledge.

Cherland, E. and Matthews, P.C. (1989) 'Attempted murder of a newborn: a case history', *Canadian Journal of Psychiatry* 34: 337–9.

Cheung, P.T.K. (1986) 'Maternal filicide in Hong Kong, 1971–85', *Medicine, Science, and the Law* 26: 185–92.

Cleaver, H. and Freeman, P. (1995) *Parental Perspectives in Cases of Suspected Child Abuse*, London: HMSO.

Coleman, R. and Cassell, D. (1995) 'Parents who misuse drugs and alcohol', in P. Reder and C. Lucey (eds) *Assessment of Parenting: Psychiatric and Psychological Contributions*, London: Routledge.

Corby, B. (1987) *Working with Child Abuse: Social Work Practice and the Child Abuse System*, Milton Keynes: Open University Press.

Crainer, S. (1993) *Zeebrugge: Learning from Disaster. Lessons on Corporate Responsibility*, London: Herald Charitable Trust.

Creighton, S.J. (1989) *Child Abuse Trends in England and Wales 1983–1987*, London: NSPCC.

—— (1992) *Child Abuse Trends in England and Wales 1988–1990: And an Overview from 1973–1990*, London: NSPCC.

—— (1995) 'Fatal child abuse – how preventable is it?', *Child Abuse Review* 4: 318–28.

Creighton, S.J. and Gallagher, B. (1988) *Child Abuse Deaths*, Information Briefing No. 5, London: NSPCC.

Creighton, S.J. and Noyes, P. (1989) *Child Abuse Trends in England and Wales 1983–1987*, London: NSPCC.

Crimmins, S., Langley, S., Brownstein, H.H. and Spunt, B.J. (1997) 'Convicted women who have killed children: a self-psychology perspective', *Journal of Interpersonal Violence* 12: 49–69.

Cronen, V.E. and Pearce, W.B. (1985) 'Toward an explanation of how the Milan method works: an invitation to a systemic epistemology and the evolution of family systems', in D. Campbell and R. Draper (eds) *Applications of Systemic Family Therapy: The Milan Approach*, London: Grune and Stratton.

Cruess, S.R. and Cruess, R.L. (1997) 'Professionalism must be taught', *British Medical Journal* 315: 1674–7.

Dale, P., Davies, M., Morrison, T. and Waters, J. (1986) *Dangerous Families: Assessment and Treatment of Child Abuse*, London: Tavistock.

Daley, M. and Wilson, M.I. (1993) 'Some differential attributes of lethal assaults on small children by stepfathers versus genetic fathers', *Ethology and Sociobiology* 15: 207–17.

Dent, R.J. (ed.) (1998) *Dangerous Care: Working to Protect Children*, London: Bridge Child Care Development Service.

Department of Health (1991) *Child Abuse: A Study of Inquiry Reports 1980–1989*, London: HMSO.

—— (1995) *Child Protection: Messages from Research*, London: HMSO.

—— (1998) *Working Together to Safeguard Children: New Government Proposals for Inter-Agency Co-operation. Consultation Paper*, Department of Health.

Department of Health and Welsh Office (1995) *Child Protection: Clarification of Arrangements Between the NHS and Other Agencies*, Department of Health.

Department of Health and Social Security (1982) *Child Abuse: A Study of Inquiry Reports 1973–1981*, London: HMSO.

Department of Health and Social Security and Welsh Office (1988) *Working Together: A Guide to Arrangements for Inter-agency Co-operation for the Protection of Children from Abuse*, London: HMSO.

Deren, S. (1986) 'Children of substance abusers: a review of the literature', *Journal of Substance Abuse Treatment* 3: 77–94.

Dingwall, R. (1986) 'The Jasmine Beckford affair', *Modern Law Review* 49: 489–507.

d'Orban, P.T. (1979) 'Women who kill their children', *British Journal of Psychiatry* 134: 560–71.

—— (1990) 'A commentary on consecutive filicide' (Review of J. Egginton's *From Cradle to Grave*), *Journal of Forensic Psychiatry* 1: 259–65.

Duncan, S. and Reder, P. (1997a) *Study of Working Together 'Part 8' Reports. The Review Process: Retrospect and Prospect*, Report to the Department of Health.

—— (1997b) 'The nature of the problem – messages from child abuse inquiries', in *Report of the 12th Annual Michael Sieff Foundation Conference 'Keeping Children in Mind: Balancing Children's Needs with Parents' Mental Health'*, Michael Sieff Foundation.

Durfee, M. (1989) 'Fatal child abuse – intervention and prevention', *Protecting Children* Spring, 9–12.

Durfee, M. and Tilton-Durfee, D. (1995) 'Multi-agency child death review teams: experiences in the United States', *Child Abuse Review* 4: 377–81.

Durfee, M.J., Gellert, G.A. and Tilton-Durfee, D. (1992) 'Origins and clinical relevance of child death review teams', *Journal of the American Medical Association* 267: 3172–5.

Eastman, N. (1996) 'Inquiry into homicides by psychiatric patients: systematic audit should replace mandatory inquiries', *British Medical Journal* 313: 1069–71.

Egan, T.G., Monaghan, S.M., Muir, R.C., Gilmore, R.J., Clarkson, J.E. and Crooks, T.J. (1990) 'Prenatal screening of pregnant mothers for parenting difficulties: final results from the Queen Mary Child Care Unit', *Social Science and Medicine* 30: 289–95.

Emery, J.L. (1985) 'Infanticide, filicide and cot death', *Archives of Disease in Childhood* 60: 505–7.

—— (1986) 'Families in which two or more cot deaths have occurred', *Lancet* i, 313–15,

—— (1993) 'Cot death and child abuse', in C.J. Hobbs and J.M. Wynne (eds) *Ballière's Clinical Paediatrics*, London: Ballière Tindall.

Etchegoyen, A. and Stubley, J. (1997) 'Nursery observation in the training of child psychiatry registrars', *Psychiatric Bulletin* 21: 156–9.

Ewigman, B., Kivlahan, C. and Land, G. (1993) 'The Missouri child fatality study: underreporting of maltreatment fatalities among children younger than five years of age, 1983 through 1986', *Pediatrics* 91: 330–7.

Falkov, A. (1996) *Study of Working Together 'Part 8' Reports. Fatal Child Abuse and Parental Psychiatric Disorder: An Analysis of 100 Area Child Protection Committee Case Reviews Conducted under the Terms of Part 8 of Working Together under the Children Act 1989*, Department of Health.

—— (1997a) 'Parental psychiatric disorder and child maltreatment. Part I: Context and historical overview'. National Children's Bureau Highlight No. 148.

—— (1997b) 'Parental psychiatric disorder and child maltreatment. Part II: Extent and nature of the association'. National Children's Bureau Highlight No. 149.

—— (1997c) 'Adult psychiatry – a missing link in the child protection network: a response to Reder and Duncan', *Child Abuse Review* 6: 41–5.

Falkov, A. and Davies, N. (1997) 'Solutions on the ground: a family mental health service?', in *Report of the 12th Annual Michael Sieff Foundation Conference 'Keeping Children in Mind: Balancing Children's Needs with Parents' Mental Health'*, Michael Sieff Foundation.

Famularo, R., Kinscherff, R. and Fenton, T. (1992) 'Parental substance abuse and the nature of child maltreatment', *Child Abuse and Neglect* 16: 475–83.

Famularo, R., Stone, K., Barnum, R. and Wharton, R. (1986) 'Alcoholism and severe child maltreatment', *American Journal of Orthopsychiatry* 56: 481–5.

Farmer, E. and Owen, M. (1995) *Child Protection Practice: Private Risks and Public Remedies – Decision Making, Intervention and Outcome in Child Protection Work*, London: HMSO.

Finnegan, P., McKinstry, E. and Robinson, G.E. (1982) 'Denial of pregnancy and childbirth', *Canadian Journal of Psychiatry* 27: 672–4.

Fitzpatrick, G. (1995) 'Assessing treatability', in P. Reder and C. Lucey (eds) *Assessment of Parenting: Psychiatric and Psychological Contributions*, London: Routledge.

Gellert, G.A., Maxwell, R.M., Durfee, M.J. and Wagner, G.A. (1995) 'Fatalities assessed by the Orange County child death review team', *Child Abuse and Neglect* 19: 875–83.

Gelles, R.J. (1991) 'Physical violence, child abuse, and child homicide: a continuum of violence, or distinct behaviors?', *Human Nature* 2: 59–72.

Gibbons, J., Gallagher, B., Bell, C. and Gordon, D. (1995) *Development after Physical Abuse in Early Childhood: A Follow-Up Study of Children on Protection Registers*, London: HMSO.

Glaser, D. and Prior, V. (1997) 'Is the term child protection applicable to emotional abuse?' *Child Abuse Review* 6: 315–29.

Göpfert, M., Webster, J. and Seeman, M.V. (eds) (1996) *Parental Psychiatric Disorder: Distressed Parents and their Families*, Cambridge: Cambridge University Press.

Gorell Barnes, G. (1985) 'Systems theory and family theory', in M. Rutter and L. Hersov (eds) *Child and Adolescent Psychiatry: Modern Approaches*, 2nd edn, Oxford: Butterworth.

Gough, D. (1995) 'The literature on child abuse fatalities: a bibliography', *Child Abuse Review* 4: 389–92.

Government Statistical Service (1997) *Children and Young People on Child Protection Registers: Year Ending 31 March 1996: England*, Department of Health.

Gray, J. and Bentovim, A. (1996) 'Illness induction syndrome: paper 1 – a series of 41 children from 37 families identified at the Great Ormond Street Hospital for Children NHS Trust', *Child Abuse and Neglect* 8: 655–73.

Green, A.H., Gaines, R.W. and Sandgrund, A. (1974) 'Child abuse: pathological syndrome of family interaction', *American Journal of Psychiatry* 131: 882–6.

Green, C.M. and Manohar, S.V. (1990) 'Neonaticide and hysterical denial of pregnancy', *British Journal of Psychiatry* 156: 121–3.

Greenland, C. (1980) 'Lethal family situations: an international comparison of deaths from child abuse', in E.J. Anthony and C. Chiland (eds) *The Child in his Family: Vol. 6: Preventive Child Psychiatry in an Age of Transition*, New York: Wiley.

—— (1987) *Preventing CAN Deaths: An International Study of Deaths Due to Child Abuse and Neglect*, London: Tavistock.

Hagell, A. (1998) *Dangerous Care: Reviewing the Risks to Children from their Carers*, London: Policy Studies Institute.

Hallett, C. (1989) 'Child abuse inquiries and public policy', in O. Stevenson (ed.) *Child Abuse: Public Policy and Professional Practice*, Hemel Hempsted: Harvester Wheatsheaf.

Hallett, C. and Birchall, E. (1992) *Coordination and Child Protection: A Review of the Literature*, Edinburgh: HMSO.

Hardy, J.B. and Streett, R. (1989) 'Family support and parenting education in the home: an effective extension of clinic-based preventive health care services for poor children', *Journal of Pediatrics* 115: 927–31.

Hawton, K., Roberts, J. and Goodwin, G. (1985) 'The risk of child abuse among mothers who attempt suicide', *British Journal of Psychiatry* 146: 486–9.

Heard, D. and Lake, B. (1997) *The Challenge of Attachment for Caregiving*, London: Routledge.

Hegar, R.L., Zuravin, S.J. and Orme, J.G. (1994) 'Factors predicting severity of physical child abuse injury: a review of the literature', *Journal of Interpersonal Violence* 9: 170–83.

Herrenkohl, R.C., Herrenkohl, E.C., Egolf, B. and Seech, M. (1979) 'The repetition of child abuse: how frequently does it occur?', *Child Abuse and Neglect* 3: 67–72.

Hicks, R.A. and Gaughan, D.C. (1995) 'Understanding fatal child abuse', *Child Abuse and Neglect* 19: 855–63.

Hobbs, C.J. and Wynne, J.M. (1996) 'Child abuse and sudden infant death', *Child Abuse Review* 5: 155–169.

Hobbs, C.J., Wynne, J.M. and Gelletlie, R. (1995) 'Leeds inquiry into infant deaths: the importance of abuse and neglect in sudden infant death', *Child Abuse Review* 4: 329–39.

Hollander, N. (1986) 'Physical abuse as a predictor of child homicide', *Texas Medicine* 82: 21–3.

Holmes, J. (1993) *John Bowlby and Attachment Theory*, London: Routledge.

Home Office, Department of Health, Department of Education and Science and Welsh Office (1991) *Working Together under the Children Act 1989: A Guide to Arrangements for Inter-agency Co-operation for the Protection of Children from Abuse*, London: HMSO.

Hunter, R.S., Kilstrom, N., Kraybill, E.N. and Loda, F. (1978) 'Antecedents of child abuse and neglect in premature infants: a prospective study in a newborn intensive care unit', *Pediatrics* 61: 629–35.

Husain, A. and Daniel, A. (1984) 'A comparative study of filicidal and abusive mothers', *Canadian Journal of Psychiatry* 29: 596–8.

Imber-Black, E. (1988) *Families and Larger Systems: A Family Therapist's Guide through the Labyrinth*, New York: Guilford.

Inquiry Report (1974) *Report of the Committee of Inquiry into the Care and Supervision Provided in Relation to Maria Colwell*, London: HMSO.

—— (1985) *A Child in Trust: The Report of the Panel of Inquiry into the Circumstances Surrounding the Death of Jasmine Beckford*, London Borough of Brent.

Jason, J. and Andereck, N.D. (1983) 'Fatal child abuse in Georgia: the epidemiology of severe physical child abuse', *Child Abuse and Neglect* 7: 1–9.

Jaudes, P.K., Ekwo, E. and van Voorhis, J. (1995) 'Association of drug abuse and child abuse', *Child Abuse and Neglect* 19: 1065–75.

Jolley, A. and Maitra, B. (in press) 'Liaison between child and adult services', in P. Reder, M. McClure and A. Jolley (eds) *Family Matters: Interfaces between Child and Adult Mental Health*, London: Routledge.

Jones, C. (1996) 'Anti-intellectualism and the peculiarities of British social work education', in N. Parton (ed.) *Social Theory, Social Change and Social Work*, London: Routledge.

Kaplun, D. and Reich, R. (1976) 'The murdered child and his killers', *American Journal of Psychiatry* 133: 809–13.

Kelley, S.J. (1992) 'Parenting stress and child maltreatment in drug-exposed children', *Child Abuse and Neglect* 16: 317–28.

Korbin, J.E. (1986) 'Childhood histories of women imprisoned for fatal child maltreatment', *Child Abuse and Neglect* 10: 331–8.

—— (1987) 'Incarcerated mothers' perceptions and interpretations of their fatally maltreated children', *Child Abuse and Neglect* 11: 397–407.

—— (1989) 'Fatal maltreatment by mothers: a proposed framework', *Child Abuse and Neglect* 13: 481–9.

Krugman, R.D. (1985) 'Fatal child abuse: analysis of 24 cases', *Pediatrician* 12: 68–72.

Lawson, M.S. and Wilson, G.S. (1980) 'Parenting among women addicted to narcotics', *Child Welfare* 59: 67–79.

Levine, M. (1996) a letter in *Child Abuse and Neglect* 20: 643–4.

Levine, M., Freeman, J. and Compaan, C. (1994) 'Maltreatment-related fatalities: issues of policy and prevention', *Law and Policy* 16: 449–71.

Loader, P. and Kelly, C. (1996) 'Munchausen syndrome by proxy: a narrative approach to explanation', *Clinical Child Psychology and Psychiatry* 1: 353–63.

Lynch, M.A. and Roberts, J. (1982) *Consequences of Child Abuse*, London: Academic Press.

McClain, P.W., Sacks, J.J., Froehlke, R.G. and Ewigman, B.G. (1993) 'Estimates of fatal child abuse and neglect, United States, 1979 through 1988', *Pediatrics* 91: 338–43.

McClure, R.J., Davis, P.M., Meadow, S.R. and Sibert, J.R. (1996) 'Epidemiology of Munchausen syndrome by proxy, non-accidental poisoning, and accidental suffocation', *Archives of Disease in Childhood* 75: 57–61.

McGoldrick, M. and Gerson, R. (1985) *Genograms in Family Assessment*, New York: Norton.

McGrath, P. (1992) 'Maternal filicide in Broadmoor Hospital: 1919–69', *Journal of Forensic Psychiatry* 3: 271–97.

Margolin, L. (1990) 'Fatal child neglect', *Child Welfare* 69: 309–19.

Marks, M.N. and Kumar, R. (1993) 'Infanticide in England and Wales', *Medicine, Science, and the Law* 33: 329–39.

—— (1996) 'Infanticide in Scotland', *Medicine, Science, and the Law* 36: 299–305.

Meadow, R. (1982) 'Munchausen syndrome by proxy', *Archives of Disease in Childhood* 57: 92–8.

Meadow, R. (1984) 'Fictitious epilepsy', *Lancet* ii: 25–8.

—— (1990) 'Suffocation, recurrent apnea, and sudden infant death', *Journal of Pediatrics* 117: 351–7.

Mogielnicki, R.P., Mogielnicki, N.P., Chandler, J.E. and Weissberg, M.P. (1977). Impending child abuse: psychosomatic symptoms in adults as a clue', *Journal of the American Medical Association* 237: 1109–11.

Murphy, J.M., Bishop, S.J., Jellineck, M.S., Quinn, D. and Poitrast, F.G. (1992) 'What happens after the care and protection petition? Reabuse in a court sample', *Child Abuse and Neglect* 16: 485–553.

Murphy, J.M., Jellinek, M., Quinn, D., Smith, G., Poitrast, F.G. and Goshko, M. (1991) 'Substance abuse and serious child mistreatment: prevalence, risk, and outcome in a court sample', *Child Abuse and Neglect* 15: 197–211.

Murphy, S., Orkow, B. and Nicola, R.M. (1985) 'Prenatal prediction of child abuse and neglect: a prospective study', *Child Abuse and Neglect* 9: 225–35.

Oates, M. (1997) 'Patients as parents: the risk to children', *British Journal of Psychiatry* 170 (suppl. 32): 22–7.

Olds, D.L., Henderson, C.R., Chamberlin, R. and Tatelbaum, R. (1986) 'Preventing child abuse and neglect: a randomized trial of nurse home visitation', *Pediatrics* 78: 65–78.

Olds, D.L., Eckenrode, J., Henderson, C.R., Kitzman, H., Powers, J., Cole, R., Sidora, K., Morris, P., Pettitt, L.M. and Luckey, D. (1997) 'Long-term effects of home visitation on maternal life course and child abuse and neglect: fifteen-year follow-up of a randomized trial', *Journal of the American Medical Association* 278: 637–43.

Oliver, J.E. (1983) 'Dead children from problem families in NE Wiltshire', *British Medical Journal* 286: 115–17.

—— (1988) 'Successive generations of child maltreatment: the children', *British Journal of Psychiatry* 153: 543–53.

Olofsson, M., Buckley, W., Anderson, G.E. and Friis-Hansen, B. (1983) 'Investigation of 89 children born by drug dependent mothers: II. Follow-up 1–10 years after birth', *Acta Paediatrica Scandinavica* 72: 407–10.

Oppenheimer, R. (1981) 'At risk: children of female psychiatric inpatients', *Child Abuse and Neglect* 5: 117–22.

Orme, T. C. and Rimmer, J. (1981) 'Alcoholism and child abuse: a review', *Journal of Studies on Alcohol* 42: 273–87.

Ounsted, C. and Lynch, M.A. (1976) 'Family pathology as seen in England', in R.E. Helfer and C.H. Kempe (eds) *Child Abuse and Neglect: The Family and the Community*, Cambridge, Mass.: Ballinger.

Ounsted, C., Roberts, J.C., Gordon, M. and Milligan, B. (1982) 'Fourth goal of perinatal medicine', *British Medical Journal* 284: 879–82.

Pearce, W.B. (1989) *Communication and the Human Condition*, Carbondale, Ill.: Southern Illinois University Press.

Pianta, R., Egeland, B. and Erickson, M.F. (1989) 'The antecedents of maltreatment: results of the mother-child interaction project', in D. Cicchetti and V. Carlson (eds) *Child Maltreatment: Theory and Research on the Causes and Consequences of Child Abuse and Neglect*, Cambridge: Cambridge University Press.

Polansky, N.A., Chalmers, M.A., Williams, D.P. and Buttenwieser, E.W. (1981) *Damaged Parents: An Anatomy of Child Neglect*, Chicago: University of Chicago.

Reder, P. (1996a) 'Child protection: medical responsibilities', *Child Abuse Review* 5: 64–6.

—— (1996b) 'Revised child protection arrangements for the health service', *Child Abuse Review* 5: 128–32.

—— (1996c) 'A management course for senior registrars', *Psychiatric Bulletin* 20: 295–7.

Reder, P. and Duncan, S. (1990) 'On meeting systems', *Human Systems* 1: 153–62.

—— (1995a) 'Closure, covert warnings and escalating child abuse', *Child Abuse and Neglect* 19: 1517–21.

—— (1995b) 'The meaning of the child', in P. Reder and C. Lucey (eds) *Assessment of Parenting: Psychiatric and Psychological Contributions*, London: Routledge.

—— (1996) 'Reflections on child abuse inquiries', in J. Peay (ed.) *Inquiries after Homicide*, London: Duckworth.

—— (1997a) *Study of Working Together 'Part 8' Reports: Practice Implications from a Review of Cases*, Report to the Department of Health.

—— (1997b) 'Adult psychiatry – a missing link in the child protection network: comments on Falkov's "Fatal Child Abuse and Parental Psychiatric Disorder" (DOH 1996)', *Child Abuse Review* 6: 35–40.

—— (1998) 'A proposed system for reviewing child abuse deaths', *Child Abuse Review* 280–6.

—— (2000) 'Predicting fatal child abuse and neglect', in K. Browne, H. Hanks and P. Stratton (eds) *The Prediction and Prevention of Child Abuse: A Handbook*, Chichester: Wiley.

Reder, P., Duncan, S. and Gray, M. (1993a) *Beyond Blame: Child Abuse Tragedies Revisited*, London: Routledge.

—— (1993b) 'Child protection dilemmas in a "not-existing" pattern of abuse', *Journal of Family Therapy* 15: 57–64.

—— (1993c) 'A new look at child abuse tragedies', *Child Abuse Review* 2: 89–100.

Reder, P., McClure, M. and Jolley, A. (eds) (in press) *Family Matters: Interfaces between Child and Adult Mental Health*, London: Routledge.

Reid, S. (ed.) (1997) *Developments in Infant Observation*, London: Routledge.

Resnick, P.J. (1969) 'Child murder by parents: a psychiatric review of filicide', *American Journal of Psychiatry* 126: 325–334.

—— (1970) 'Murder of the newborn: a psychiatric review of neonaticide', *American Journal of Psychiatry* 126: 1414–20.

Roberts, J. (1988) 'Why are some families more vulnerable to child abuse?', in K. Browne, C. Davies and P. Stratton (eds) *Early Prediction and Prevention of Child Abuse*, Chichester: Wiley.

Roberts, J. and Hawton, K. (1980) 'Child abuse and attempted suicide', *British Journal of Psychiatry* 137: 319–23.

Rutter, M. and Quinton, D. (1984) 'Parental psychiatric disorder: effects on children', *Psychological Medicine* 14: 853–80.

Sabotta, E.E. and Davis, R.L. (1992) 'Fatality after report to a child abuse registry in Washington State, 1973–1986', *Child Abuse and Neglect* 16: 627–35.

Saunders, E. (1989) 'Neonaticide following "secret" pregnancies: seven case reports', *Public Health Reports* 104: 368–72.

Schloesser, P., Pierpoint, J. and Poertner, J. (1992) 'Active surveillance of child abuse fatalities', *Child Abuse and Neglect* 16: 3–10.

Schmitt, B.D. and Krugman, R.D. (1992) 'Abuse and neglect of children', in R.E. Behrman (ed.) *Nelson Textbook of Pediatrics*, 14th edn, Philadelphia: Saunders.

Scott, P.D. (1973) 'Fatal battered baby cases', *Medicine, Science, and the Law* 13: 197–206.

Showers, J., Apolo, J., Thomas, J. and Beavers, S. (1985) 'Fatal child abuse: a two-decade review', *Pediatric Emergency Care* 1: 66–70.

Smith, G. (1993) *Systemic Approaches to Training in Child Protection*, London: Karnac.

Soumenkoff, C., Marneffe, C., Gerard, M., Limet, R., Beeckmans, M. and Hubinont, P.O. (1982) 'A coordinated attempt for prevention of child abuse at the antenatal care level', *Child Abuse and Neglect* 6: 87–94.

Southall, D.P., Plunkett, M.C.B., Banks, M.W., Falkov, A.F. and Samuels, M.P. (1997) 'Covert video recordings of life-threatening child abuse: lessons for child protection', *Pediatrics* 100: 735–60.

Southall, D.P., Stebbens, V.A., Rees, S.V., Lang, M.H., Warner, J.O. and Shinebourne, E.A. (1987) 'Apnoeic episodes induced by smothering: two cases identified by covert video surveillance', *British Medical Journal* 294: 1637–41.

Starr, R.H. (1988) 'Pre- and perinatal risk and physical abuse', *Journal of Reproductive and Infant Psychology* 6: 125–38.

Steele, B. (1980) 'Psychodynamic factors in child abuse', in C.H. Kempe and R.E. Helfer (eds) *The Battered Child*, 3rd edn, Chicago: University of Chicago Press.

Steering Committee (1996) *Report of the Confidential Inquiry into Homicides and Suicides by Mentally Ill People*, London: Royal College of Psychiatrists.

Stewart, D. and Gangbar, R. (1984) 'Psychiatric assessment of competency to care for a new-born', *Canadian Journal of Psychiatry* 29: 583–9.

Stewart, J. (1995) 'The toughest homicides of all', *Los Angeles Times Magazine* July 16: 11–15 and 30.

Stratton, P., Preston-Shoot, M. and Hanks, H. (1990) *Family Therapy: Training and Practice*, Birmingham: Venture Press.

Swadi, H. (1994) 'Parenting capacity and substance misuse: an assessment scheme', *ACPP Review and Newsletter* 16: 237–44.

Taylor, C.G., Norman, D.K., Murphy, J.M., Jellinek, M., Quinn, D., Poitrast, F.G. and Goshko, M. (1991) 'Diagnosed intellectual and emotional impairment among parents who seriously mistreat their children: prevalence, type, and outcome in a court sample', *Child Abuse and Neglect* 15: 389–401.

Taylor, R. (1989) *The Hillsborough Stadium Disaster: Interim Report*, London: HMSO.

Thorburn, J., Lewis, A. and Shemmings, D. (1995) *Paternalism or Partnership? Family Involvement in the Child Protection Process*, London: HMSO.

Tuteur, W. and Glotzer, J. (1966) 'Further observations on murdering mothers', *Journal of Forensic Sciences* 11: 373–83.

US Advisory Board on Child Abuse and Neglect (1995) *A Nation's Shame: Fatal Child Abuse and Neglect in the United States*, Washington: Department of Health and Human Services.

Vietze, P.M., O'Connor, S., Sherrod, K.B. and Altemeier, W.A. (1991) 'The early screening project', in R.H. Starr and D.A. Wolfe (eds) *The Effects of Child Abuse and Neglect*, New York: Guilford.

Watzlawick, P., Weakland, J. and Fisch, R. (1974) *Change: Principles of Problem Formation and Problem Resolution*, New York: Norton.

Webb, D. (1996) 'Regulation for radicals: the state, CCETSW and the academy', in N. Parton (ed.) *Social Theory, Social Change and Social Work*, London: Routledge.

Whiffen, R. and Byng-Hall, J. (eds) (1982) *Family Therapy Supervision: Recent Developments in Practice*, London: Academic Press.

Whipple, E.E. and Webster-Stratton, C. (1991) 'The role of parental stress in physically abusive families', *Child Abuse and Neglect* 15: 279–91.

Wilczynski, A. (1991) 'Images of women who kill their infants: the mad and the bad', *Women and Criminal Justice* 2: 71–88.

—— (1994) 'The incidence of child homicide: how accurate are the official statistics?', *Journal of Clinical Forensic Medicine* 1: 61–6.

—— (1995) 'Risk factors for parental child homicide: results of an English study', *Current Issues in Criminal Justice* 7: 193–222.

—— (1997) *Child Homicide*, London: Greenwich Medical Media.

Wilkey, I., Pearn, J., Petrie, G. and Nixon, J. (1982) 'Neonaticide, infanticide and child homicide', *Medicine, Science, and the Law* 22: 241–53.

Wilkins, A.J. (1985) 'Attempted infanticide', *British Journal of Psychiatry* 146: 206–8.

Wilson, G.S. (1989) 'Clinical studies of infants and children exposed prenatally to heroin', *Annals of New York Academy of Sciences* 562: 183–94.

Wilson, L.M., Reid, A.J., Midmer, D.K., Biringer, A., Carroll, J.C. and Stewart, D.E. (1996) 'Antenatal psychosocial risk factors associated with adverse postpartum family outcomes', *Canadian Medical Association Journal* 154: 785–99.

Wilson, M. and Daley, M. (1987) 'Risk of maltreatment of children living with stepparents', in R.J. Gelles and J.B. Lancaster (eds) *Child Abuse and Neglect: Biosocial Dimensions*, New York: Aldine de Gruyter.

Wood, J.M. (1997) 'Risk prediction for re-abuse or re-neglect in a predominantly Hispanic population', *Child Abuse and Neglect* 21: 379–89.

Woodhouse, D. and Pengelly, P. (1991) *Anxiety and the Dynamics of Collaboration*, Aberdeen: Aberdeen University Press.

Young, L. (1964) *Wednesday's Children: A Study of Child Neglect and Abuse*, New York: McGraw-Hill.

Author index

Note: page numbers in italics refer to tables or figures

Subject index

Note: Page numbers in italics denote figures or tables where these are separated from the textual reference

DATE	ISSUED TO
11/15/10	